1

AN INTRODUCTION: LIFE BEFORE THE SPORT

I grew up in a suburb north of Houston called Spring, Texas.

We used to watch fights growing up at my dad's friend's place from the Houston Police Department.

He was a former boxer from New York and former paid sparring partner of Mike Tyson. He asked me if I wanted to try out boxing one day and took me to a gym.

I'd played baseball and basketball up to my sophomore and junior year in high school.

After my first session at the gym I was hooked. I told my high school basketball and baseball coaches that I was quitting to pursue boxing to which they found amusing.

The first six weeks in the gym, my nose would bleed at least once a week in sparring. The gym owner and trainer, Willie Savannah, would come out of his office and say, "Cot dammit! Can't be bleeding all over the ring every day."

My trainer told me to snort vinegar. It would burn so bad but my bleeding went away.

I was driving 30-45 minutes every day after school during peak Houston traffic to bust my nose and snort acetic acid.

My first fight was at rap mogul J Princes' Boxing Explosion in Houston 2002 in my junior year and I won by TKO first round.

I had no idea what I was getting into. I didn't know the feeling of jitters.

That fight was the only fight I didn't think at all about what was going to happen. I just approached it like previous sports and just went out and competed.

Through a few more amateur boxing matches, I met MMA Pioneer Yves Edwards. He introduced me to grappling and Muay Thai. He had a gym a lot closer to me than the boxing gyms so I did a lot of my training with him. Yves was

MUAY THAI GRIT

STORIES OF AN AMERICAN NAK MUAY

MICHAEL CHASE CORLEY

top 5 in the world and I was able to travel with him and learn the ropes of the fight game from the fights at Indian reservations in California, to UFC's, all the way to Pride Fighting Championship in Japan all by the age of 21. I got to travel with Yves and the team everywhere and took a lot of educational beatings along the way.

Yves introduced me to so many people in this game. I still seek advice from many like boxing legends Lewis Wood, Kenny Weldon (RIP), MMA coaches Saul Soliz, Tim Creduer, and for Muay Thai, Saekson.

I had my first two Muay Thai fights at Saekson Janjira's gym. One was a bout against a fighter from his gym. The second was against a local fighter from another school.

I remember being nervous fighting one of his guys. In the lobby of his gym where we were checking our weight it had a highlight video playing of Saekson breaking legs with his kicks and Pete Spratt, one of his top students, smashing pads. It scared the hell out of me.

He called Yves "Tae Bo" and said I was welcome to come train with him anytime. It was through Saekson that I learned real Muay Thai. I would occasionally drive four hours to Dallas to train with him throughout my senior year in high school and college. Yves knew I took a liking to Muay Thai and encouraged it.

The first time I did a private lesson with Saekson I was so nervous, I slipped and fell just shadow boxing a kick.

I didn't know about the Thai liniment that boxers put on their body to warm up, hell I didn't even own a pair of Thai trunks when I went for my first fight. I bought some of his school shorts and fought one of their own guys in them.

Yves moved to Florida to train at American Top Team and I headed off to college at Texas A&M University about an hour and a half away from Houston.

Throughout college, I would drive to Houston a lot of

weekends to train because there was not any high level training there at the time other than the Bryan Boxing Club.

During my time in college it was hard to get matches in anything Muay Thai so I focused back on my boxing and won the Sub Novice Golden Gloves, and after that I won six straight matches in boxing. During that time, I even did a couple MMA smokers.

I kept at my training returning home to Houston after graduating with a degree in Sport Management. I was in limbo of what I would do with myself, real job or pursue fighting?

To add to the confusion my girlfriend at the time and I split. I went to a Texas Talent Search for consideration for the USA Muay Thai Team. I did pretty well and submitted a tape of training. I made the USA Team for the Olympics of Muay Thai, the IFMA World Championship in Busan, Korea.

That moment changed my life. I was good nationally but there was another level to the international game.

Arriving in Korea and taking buses around as a USA Team Athlete felt like I'd made it.

At the first meeting we all introduced ourselves and met the coach of the team Kirian Fitzgibbons.

We were issued our USA Track Suits, and I'm not going to lie, I wore that thing around everywhere. I was so excited to represent. I roomed with fellow Texan, Daniel Kim. We talked about our different backgrounds and how tough it is to maintain good training in Texas in this sport.

The first day of fights the gymnasium was full of athletes warming up and menthol in the air from the Thai liniment. The cracking of pads, the smell was all something different to anything I experienced. It was international.

I actually questioned if I was ready. I was just chilling, sitting down and Coach Kirian must have had a read on me and came by to talk.

"Hey man, don't just sit back out here in the back watching everyone hit pads. Go out and watch the fights."

Kirian had a calm tone to his voice. He had a switch that he could light an electricity into a fighter, but for me, right then, no spark was needed. His voice soothed.

I took his advice.

I started watching the B Class ring where I was going to compete and saw that I did in fact belong and I needed to relax. To this day at international tournaments I always tell the USA athletes I oversee to go watch the fights to put them at ease.

It was my day to fight. I was against New Zealand. My young philosophy of Muay Thai scoring at the time, was to just damage my opponent and/or get him out. I thought I had done just that.

I scored a knockdown but I also ate a lot of kicks along the way. The last round my coach said, "Mike you got the fight, just add some kicks in there this round."

When the decision came I had lost. I didn't understand, but looking back I wasn't displaying a lot of Muay Thai. I was boxing my way through.

Looking throughout the tournament I noticed all of our USA Athletes were in the B division. I wanted to see what the A was about and watched some of the bouts. It was a whole different level, the timing, the balance, everything.

The USA Team that year only had eight people and I think only a couple of Bronze for B. I had my goals set on leveling up and one day fighting A Class. I was told that no one from the USA has competed in the A class since they separated divisions.

The President at the time of USA Muay Thai offered any of the team members 25% off if they went to train at Fairtex Bangplee, Thailand. Fairtex Bangplee had a lot of history, and is where Lumpinee champions Bunkerd, Neungsiam,

Yoknoi, and Jongsanan all came from. Next door to the camp is where the Fairtex equipment was made.

I was the first to volunteer and within a couple of weeks of returning home from Korea I had set off for Thailand.

2

MY FIRST TASTE OF REAL
MUAY THAI

The Fairtex camp boss came into the dining hall.

"You all need to be in the lobby at four. The van will pick you up," he said.

"There are big fights at Lumpinee."

I was going to see one of the sports all-time greats, Saenchai, in his prime, in the mecca of Muay Thai, Lumpinee Stadium.

Within the first few days of arriving I was off to watch kids at the camp compete at a fight at the temple. Temple fights were outdoor set ups with tons of food stalls, games, lights and loud traditional Isaan music. The fights were generally kids, up and comers, and occasionally a big bet fight with gyms, but now I was going to where the elite fought, Lumpinee. It was a major educational experience.

The crowd was electric, there were gamblers filled to the rafters. They were climbing on top of each other, packed together like sardines in a tin can. The outside walls of the stadium looked normal but inside the roof was a tin metal roof and had a smell of rust. Surrounding the ring were floor seats reserved for foreign tourists and VIPs while the majority of the crowd was in the rafters and where the legal gambling took place.

Every strike the crowd rumbled.

The legend, Saenchai, was fighting Saenchainoi Toyotarayong and was backing up the whole time, playing a counter game.

He was landing less strikes but very clear shots. In the fourth round, in my head it was really close, in the last ten seconds of the round Saenchai offsets his opponent in the clinch and breaks his posture. He placed a knee and held it there and the crowd went crazy.

Something changed in the stadium.

"What's going on," I asked the camp boss.

"That's it. He's got it."

I started seeing people emptying out and even though there was still the fifth round left. The last round started and Saenchanoi pressured and threw hard shots but nothing landed really effectively. They both backed off and danced off the round. I thought Saenchanois forward aggression was winning but boy was I wrong. I didn't know shit about scoring.

The next morning my trainer basically gave me a tutorial in Thai stadium scoring. I really didn't know anything.

It was something that I aimed to improve on during the course of my career in the sport. A lot of people compete in Muay Thai but don't understand it. I continually tried to learn as much as I could through referee and judge courses.

My trainer at that time was Fonduod. He was about 5'8 but very strong Thai-Malay from southern Thailand. He was the only Muslim trainer in the camp. He wasn't a drinker like the other trainers but he loved to gamble. He knew everything there was to scoring.

Every morning before training he would mix an instant coffee and read Muay Siam, the daily Muay Thai paper.

I'd gotten a taste of real Muay Thai in Thailand but my time was short. I wanted more.

You get a month when you visit Thailand as an American, and at that time anything else would require a visa. My time was up. I got some contacts from some of the other international fighters there and made my way to the airport. I was motivated. I had seen the Thai kids train, I had seen a sponsored foreign fighters train, I saw one of the greats in Lumpinee, and had a better grasp on what real Muay Thai was. All I wanted to do was go home and save money to get back to Thailand.

There wasn't anywhere in the USA that could mimic the training.

Every morning the roosters would wake up everyone at the camp for the run. After a run, there would be a little cooling down before jumping rope for 15 minutes. The training area was around 3,000 square feet of outdoor covered training. It was hot all year round.

Seniority was based on how much time people had been at the camp.

They were the first to get pad work. A typical day of pad work would be five rounds of Muay Thai and two rounds of boxing if you were in good condition. Before or after, pads would be bag work and trainers really saw what your intentions were based on how you worked on the bags.

Afternoon sessions would have another jog if you were losing weight for a fight or just really trying to get fit. When all of the pad and bag work was done the clinching or sparring started. A lot of the tourists never wanted to clinch and would play spar with the trainers. If you were competing, clinching was mandatory. Thai kids that were only 12 or 13 years old from the camp would rag doll grown men with their technique. They would use the foreigners' aggression and dump them on the ground. I learned so much from these kids. Most of the kids at the camp had over 50 professional fights and were not even 16.

Outdoor training, trainers, pad work, and Muay Thai fights every day.

I knew that if I had any shot in doing this at elite level it had to be here in Thailand.

3

RETURNING HOME

Houston is a huge city. There are no trains or subways and the bus routes are crazy. Everyone drives everywhere and a lot of the gyms are spread out.

Training Muay Thai in Houston was tough. There weren't enough athletes solely dedicated to Muay Thai in the city. I would round up some people for sparring on Saturdays but during the week it was hard to get pad work or any kind of solid work.

As I was settling back into Spring, (a suburb north of Houston) I began to look for an apartment.

Some close friends from high school were looking to get

an apartment as well. Four of us ended up getting an apartment next door to each other in the Spring-Woodlands area of North Houston.

There was a Gracie Barra just down the street from the apartment and a boxing gym across the street. It seemed like it would be a good place to be for Muay Thai, but it just wasn't enough.

I was frustrated with training, teaching classes, working at a golf course, and taking odd jobs to make money. I had a bachelor's degree in sport management from Texas A&M and was trying my best to avoid getting a 9-5 type job.

I began to fall into a bad routine where I was either BBQing or just drinking too many nights of the week. Sunday was a bad day because the golf course we all worked at was closed on Mondays. We would hit it hard.

It was a good four to six months of time of just working and saving money and not being in a good routine. I was seeing athletes from my 2008 USA Team staying active in California and New York. I was seeing friends from high school settle into careers and getting married and I was bouncing around town trying to be a "fighter."

I was down. I had a small taste of what it's like to be elite in the sport and I was back home just wasting time. I made a lot of bad decisions during that period related to drinking. It's like the saying, "Idle hands are the devil's work," and without any fights in the books I was contemplating if this was something I should still try for. It had been seven or eight months since I competed.

One day I saw a post in a forum or something online from Mike Miles in Canada. He is one of Canada's pioneers for Muay Thai. He competed and coached at a high level and promoted shows. He said he needed someone for a 165lb fight against his fighter Peter Arbeu, but the bout was in two weeks. I agreed to the bout right away without even looking up his record. I had zero fights since IFMA and if it wasn't for this opportunity I don't think I would have continued with this journey.

"It will be the co-main event," he said. "Full rules Muay Thai and five rounds."

"Since it's short notice, can we do three rounds," I asked.

He agreed. The bout was set for me in Calgary.

As soon as I got off the phone I looked up my opponent on google and found that he was the #1 amateur in the IKF rankings and had won numerous championships. He had over 30 fights and I had just 15 or so. It didn't matter because with the year I was having there was no way I wasn't going to win this fight.

I took my boxing coach at the time, Lewis Wood, with me. He stood at a height of five foot five and every inch of him was no nonsense. His eyes were mean and serious. I don't think I ever saw him laugh. We were focused. We were heading into a hometown crowd. At the weigh ins I met Mike Miles and I knew him from being one of Canada's coaches for IFMA. He was happy I took the fight.

I weighed in and everything was good to go. It was my first fight without shin guards, and oddly I wasn't worried at all.

Fight day and I was in the back telling Lewis how this whole Muay Thai thing works. I told him I have to put on this *mongkol* and seal the ring, and do a little dance and come back. After that you will remove the *mongkol*. Just imagine telling that to the hardest boxer you've ever met.

He just stared at me and snarled "Ok, Man."

The place was packed and the crowd was educated. Every clean strike was a, "Oaaa," like in Thailand. It was pretty unique to have that kind of following in Calgary, but Mike has been doing shows for years.

I didn't pick a walk out song and boy should I. I never

cared about walk out songs and walk out t-shirts. They had me coming out to Phil Collins, "I can feel it coming in the air tonight."

It must have been mind games because I was like, what the fuck is this? The crowd was all looking at me funny. I entered the ring and waited for my opponent. The crowd got loud for the hometown fighter. The music began with the *wai kru* and I did a very simple *wai kru*.

The *wai kru* is the pre-fight dance ritual in the ring where fighters pay respects to their teachers, camp, and family. After the *wai kru* the fighters are brought to the center by the referee for instructions and then they go to their corners to have the coach remove the *mongkol*.

The *mongkol* is a blessed headband worn to the ring and during *wai kru*. Can you imagine an old school boxer's face seeing all this right before the fight? I went over to the corner and bowed my head and I told Lewis to act like he's praying over me and remove the *mongkol*. He had a face like he had done this thousands of times and we were off.

Round one began and I realized that my boxing is what's going to win me this fight. When he would kick or throw anything I was countering with three punches at least. Round one was mine. Round two I started getting comfortable and knowing that I was in someone else's backyard I started to add a little flair to get the crowd going. I was throwing spinning backfist, jumping knees, and jumping spike elbows. Each move was getting a rise from the crowd. The fight was close but I think I just had more volume. I didn't get tired. I didn't sit in the corner. I stood and listened to Lewis. He did a sort of back hand to your chest to make sure I was paying attention. He would give the directions in a calm yet almost fearful way. You didn't want that man mad. Round three I was still at it.

The bell rang and I went back to my corner happy. They

brought the two of us to the center and I was awarded the winner by split decision.

The crowd was so cool, I had people come up and buy me a beer. It's not often you make Lewis proud and on that day I think I did. He watched me have a few beers and then the fighters were shuttled back to the host hotel. There was an old bar in the basement and a bunch of us went down for a few.

When I came back home everyone wanted to celebrate. It was pretty cool, everyone was excited that I won and had seen it on Facebook. That was the first time I felt I accomplished something decent in the sport. All I was thinking about though was getting back to Thailand. This was good, but I knew I was still very far behind what I saw on that trip.

2009 IFMA

A couple weeks went by and I shot a message out to the USA Team about me being on the team for 2009. They had heard about my win in Canada.

They said yes, but that year there was a larger team and some of the spots were already taken. Many of the athletes and team coaches were from the West Coast and a lot of those athletes had a lot more experience than a nobody from Texas, but hey I just got a big win. I was going to throw my hat in the ring.

They told me that my division was taken in the B class, which was for lower experienced pros and high level amateurs, and said all that was left was A class. A class was a four round fight with the world's best pros. Not only that, the division that was my weight had a ton of athletes in it. Since I was still an amateur they recommended I go up another division to 81kg. The highest I had ever fought and would ever fight in Muay Thai. My first draw was against a lengthy Morrocan who had gained a lot of experience in Europe and primarily the Netherlands.

The fights took place at the Mall Bangkapi in Bangkok. It was a huge mall with multiple levels. The top floor was a huge convention center set up with multiple rings and a little Muay Thai shopping area upon entering. It was similar to a festival fight and that it was all out in the open just under a roof.

There were no locker rooms, each team would find a spot each day and set all of our bags down. Fighters would warm up with all eyes on them.

First round I came out guns blazing and did pretty well. The second round the much bigger fighter started using his range and landed a great knee right on my chin which split me open. The Moroccan went on to win rounds three and four using his length and taking the decision.

After the fight I had to go to the hospital to get stitched up. It was just eight stitches on the chin, and a small bag of what I thought were pain relievers. I was rushing through the hospital to make it back to watch the rest of the USA Team fight.

I made it back to the venue, grabbed a Gatorade and

popped a couple of "pain relievers." I was sitting there watching the fights and I started seeing all kinds of crazy stuff. The Thai fight music was gonzo and the fighters were floating in the ring. I was really freaking out. I checked the bottle of pills that they had given me at the hospital and they were muscle relaxers not pain relievers.

I must have had a bad reaction to them because I got pale white and all the fighters in the ring were floating around and fighting. After the fights I went home and slept it off for a bit.

I woke up late in the night and made my rounds around the hotel where a bunch of the eliminated fighters from all around the world are drinking and discussing what debauchery they were getting into in Bangkok. It was pretty funny. You don't need to speak the same language as someone to know they feel like shit after a loss and need a beer to ease the loss.

I found a couple of USA guys that got eliminated and they asked me if I was sticking around in Thailand after the World Championships. I originally had planned to go home a couple days after the tournament.

"I don't know yet, what are you guys up," I asked.

"We're going to Isaan to visit Jongsanan Fairtex's home village. We might fight," one of them said.

It was music to my ears. The next morning after our team meeting I asked Jongsanan about going to the rural north east where he was from.

"No prob bob," he said.

THE WOODEN MAN

I still had my stitches in. The cut hadn't healed. The pain had been dulled by "pain pills," that's what they call muscle relaxers in Thailand. It was pitch dark.

Jongsanan, golden era Muay Thai legend, had no idea where the hell we were.

I didn't expect to be lost in the middle of nowhere. I also didn't intend on getting hurt in the middle of nowhere.

Before we left we had a few days after the tournament so we trained at Fairtex Bangplee. A lot of the trainers told me not to fight because it had only been three days since I got my stitches. The training was good though. Jongsanan, or Noom, kept telling me I should drop weight for a better chance to get matched up.

He rented a big van and we all piled in. There were five of us and it was packed. We had to take all of our luggage from the whole trip with us. The bags filled up every inch of the van and our limbs stuck through the holes.

After a few hours of driving through the night we finally made it to Chaiyaphoom. It was dark so Noom kept missing the turn and got lost. It took us an extra hour at least and made my head and stitches ache.

We finally made it to his parents' house late at night. We woke up early the next day. Noom's house is big for an Isaan house.

A lot of buildings out there are just a couple slaps of wood and a tin roof. Jongsanan had sent money home during his fight career and he'd built a good house for his parents. His dad, who was thin as a skeleton, and his mom, who was as big as his father was thin, lived well in the house. Behind the house were rice fields as far as the eye could see.

Next door to Noom's parent's house was a small covered ring area with a bag hanging. There was a dingy carpet there too. The ends of the carpet frayed upward and it was thin as a piece of wet paper. Locals were putting up net walls for a perimeter and vendors were setting up food stands.

"Is this where we're fighting," I asked Noom.

"Yeah man," he said with a laugh.

His voice was fast, almost too fast. As he spoke, he switched back and forth between Thai and English. His round face was lined with scars but there was always a smirk across his face.

A lot of the locals came up to us and stared us down. They talked in Thai. Some of them had never seen a foreigner before.

As the day wore on more and more people began filing over to the area. Noom was a superstar returning home.

Everyone wanted to have a beer with him or take a pull of some whiskey. His breath smelled of booze when he told us to weigh in.

"Get on the scales," Noom told us.

We weighed in but there were no other fighters.

"Where are our opponents," I asked.

"Don't worry they come," he said.

When he told us not to worry all of us started to worry. Then a random guy came over, sized us up, then whispered something to Noom.

"I think we are going to get fed to the locals," I told the others.

Noom walked over to us. "Everybody good, everybody got a match. Go rest. We fight tonight."

Noom's sister had a hair salon built into the house. The salon had a few chairs and you could see the ring even while sitting on the chairs. There were combs and brushes laid out on the counters. We stayed in there until the fights started. The floor was nicer and tiled.

Noom eventually came in.

"Your guy no fight," he told Daniel Kim. He pointed at myself, Taylor and Tyler.

"You still fight."

"Who am I fighting," I asked.

"I don't know. Get ready," he said.

"What the fuck am I doing here," I asked myself. "I'm in

the middle of nowhere and no one knows what the fuck is going on."

We all started throwing on our trunks and wrapping our own hands. Noom was the biggest thing to ever come out of the village and was the center of attention. It was hard to get him back to our corner at the hair salon, to get an idea of when we were fighting. Taylor and I threw our bags under some things and found a bottle of Thai brandy. It was Regency which is sickly sweet and usually chased down with soda water or Coke. It's good when it goes down but gives you a massive hangover the next day.

Taylor and I were so nervous we both took a couple of shots to calm the nerves, not exactly allowed by the athletic commissions back home.

"You up," Noom said to Taylor. The legend was slightly loose.

We all had to fight, no warm up, nothing. Taylor entered the ring and so did his opponent. The local Thai boxer didn't seem much of a threat to Taylor. The Thai guy was small, the type of guy that hangs out by the one motorbike stand in the village all day, nothing to do. The fights started and it was evident Taylor was the stronger fighter. He did his job and got rid of his opponent quickly in the first round. We were all pumped. We were jumping around celebrating when we saw some other foreigners. Two of the foreigners were warming up hitting pads.

"What the hell are these foreigners doing way the hell out of here in this desolate place," I asked Noom.

"You are fighting that one," he said. He pointed at a fit dude covered in *sak yant*, traditional Thai tattoos. "He is from France. Training and fighting in Isaan just little bit."

"Great. First pro fight I have no idea who this guy is," I said aloud.

Noom ignored me.

I walked up to the glove table to get my mitts. The official handed me the most beat to shit pair of gloves I had ever seen. The laces were browned and tattered, barely even had strings. The edges of the gloves were as tattered as the paper thin carpet.

I could barely get my hand in the left glove as it was too small. I checked the glove sizes again and the left was a 6oz glove and the right was an 8oz! Concerned I walked back to the official and held the gloves up to him.

"*Mai bpen rai,*" he said to me, waving me along.

I managed to squeeze my hands in the gloves and get them tied up. It was time to fight. I entered the ring and prepared to do the *wai kru*. The ringside commentators kept describing me as "Cowboy," and my opponent as "*Farangset.*"

"Do I need to do the full *wai kru,*" I asked Noom as I walked into the ring.

"No. Just seal the ring," he said.

As I sealed the ring going to each corner while walking along the ring with my glove on the top rope. The act was supposed to keep out any bad spirits, the sport is steeped in tradition. I bowed to my opponent's corner. I noticed my opponent started to do a really nice *wai kru*. The ceremonial dance is a way for the fighter to pay respect to their teacher, gym, and parents. It's also a good way to get some of the pre-fight jitters out and to stretch a bit.

Back in the day people used to judge a fighter's abilities by their *wai kru*. He was real clean.

The crowd was shouting and getting their bets ready. Noom told me later that the crowd thought I was scared and didn't know the *wai kru*, the odds got up to five to one against me.

The round started and we began slowly feeling each other out. There was about 30 seconds left in the first round and the guy all of a sudden turned it up 120%. He teed off on my lead leg. After the fourth kick landed I raised my leg to block and it caught me right off my knee cap. My leg just about gave out at the end of the round. I was in serious pain walking over to the corner. As I was in the corner I saw Taylor on the ground level shouting instructions. I looked around in my corner and no one was there for water or instruction. Noom was in the crowd gambling with the locals, drinking a beer. He made eye contact with me and ran real quick up to the ring.

"Hey man you losing! You need to block low kick! Just punch him, you punch hard," he screamed at me.

"Ok, hey you got any water," I asked.

"No man sorry. Block low kick."

He returned to the crowd to keep gambling.

Round two started and he came right after my leg. He landed on it but I came back with a huge right and started throwing on him. He started backing up and I started throwing big knees. The crowd went crazy.

"Cowboy! Cowboy," the commentator screamed.

I landed a big uppercut and he turned away. I began to elbow him repeatedly and the ref broke us. On the break he began walking to the corner. My opponent waved at his cornermen to stop the bout.

I won the fight.

After the win I could barely walk and was limping around everywhere. All of the locals were giving me a weird stare. Noom came up to me and told me that the village thought that he had tricked them. The villagers thought that I had thrown the first round on purpose to get everyone to gamble on the French fighter. I legitimately got whipped in the first round. The villagers were upset with Noom because he bet on me and they thought that it was a big set up.

We went spear fishing the next day. I could barely walk. All the Thais got fish.

Us foreigners came up empty. That night, we were going to have a BBQ but needed to go pick up the pig. Because of strong buddhist beliefs, no one wanted to slaughter the pig for the BBQ. Noom told us we had to drive over to the town's "Bad Man." According to Noom, the village's designated butcher is called the "Bad Man," I don't know why he was called that. He did all the slaughtering for the town. Noom said he got paid pretty well for it.

The Thai's started BBQing the pig and throwing some other things on the pit. I walked over and saw something split in half with a tail on the grill.

"Is that a rat," I asked. They all started laughing.

"Don't worry. These field rats. Eat rice. They are clean. No disease," the bungalow owner said.

He handed me a stick with a skewered rat on it. I took a bite. It was like a gamey chicken.

"Not bad," I told the owner.

As with most Thai BBQs there was a ton of Thai whiskey and brandy at the BBQ. My knee was still killing me so I sat down, elevated my leg and enjoyed my rat and whiskey. The Thais were so accommodating they kept mixing me drinks and bringing me over plates. The bungalow owner came up to me with Noom and handed me a vial of what looked like vaseline but smelled of wood. He told me that the liquid has been extracted from the antlers of deer that roam the mountain area of Chaiyaphum. He told me that when the deer shed their antlers they will go up and pick them up to use as a healing ointment.

"When deer fall in mountains and break leg, deer lick leg. Make bone heal fast," he said pointing at his tongue. "Same same as antler. This blessed at temple."

He handed me the vial.

"Makes sense to me," I said. I was sold.

I tried it and rubbed the balm on my knee. It was like a

melted vaseline and gooped all over my joint. It didn't do much to make me feel better but the alcohol did.

When we got back to Bangkok my knee was still killing me. I went in for x-rays and they showed that I'd cracked my patella in half. The doctor said the split in my knee cap was too big to just stabilize. I'd have to let it heal. He told me it would need to be pinned together in surgery.

"That is not an option right now," I told him.

I got some Ibuprofen and went back to the camp. I had to keep fighting.

6

FIGHTING AT LUMPINEE STADIUM

A fter a couple days back wobbling around the Fairtex camp It was time for me to head back to Houston. I went to the camp manager Mark. I kept telling him how I wanted his job and asked if there were other applicants. Mark was going to leave the job to go back to school.

He had heard from the then president that they were going to offer me the job!

I was so excited. I got on a call with the president and he had told me that he was taking more of the responsibility of the Fairtex Bangplee Camp and the founder of Fairtex Mr. Wong would be working on Fairtex Pattaya. It was arranged that I was going to make 15,000 baht a month ($450 - $500), a boxer's room, eat two times a day with the boxers, and train once in the afternoon. It was a dream come true.

It wasn't going to be an easy job, but I enjoyed a challenge. A lot of the well known Fairtex fighters at the time were moved to Fairtex Pattaya under the guidance of Mr. Wong. Bangplee had history, but no longer had the stars. My job was to bring people back and attract new customers.

I flew back the next day and told all my friends and family. Not many could believe it. My parents were surprisingly supportive and all my friends really didn't care or understand? Maybe both. It was that weird age where Texas norms were for you to be in a "real job" and settle down. For me, I had just begun on a journey that took me to the other side of the world.

I cleared everything out of my apartment and took it to my parents' house. I listed all my furniture in online ads and sold it. I even sold my prized Olhausen 8 foot cherry pool table. I left to Thailand with around $2500 to my name.

My first month was just getting to know everyone behind the scenes and figuring out the system. The trainers at the time seemed cool with me being the manager and remembered me from past visits.

Mr. Wong, sent me to Cambodia after my first 30 days to get my visa stamped. He said if I did good for the next 60 days I would be getting a work visa and not have to do visa runs anymore.

It took me a little bit to get in a groove of balancing both work and training at the camp. The morning sessions at Fairtex were from 7am to 9am and the afternoon sessions 3pm to 5pm. I was up every morning before training to make sure the trainers were ready and to give a run down on the training to new people. I didn't train in the mornings due to this.

For a good part of my time at the gym I would run in the morning and do my Muay Thai in the afternoon. Eating Thai food every day and training outdoors was getting my body in shape fast.

After about a month and a half at the camp the trainers asked if I wanted to go fight at Thepprasit Stadium in Pattaya.

"Who is my opponent," I asked.

"Easy fight. No problem," my trainer said.

"Ok. Sure."

It was my first of many trips fighting in Pattaya to stay busy and sharp. At that point I'd only had one fight in Thailand. My second fight was against a Thai trainer at one of the gyms in Pattaya. The bout wasn't much trouble and I stopped him in the third round. It was one of the ones where I didn't even take a photo or video just in and out. It was right back to work at the camp the next day. Funny thing is, some people go over and fight a similar level fighter or even a tuk tuk driver and think they are a world champion.

I guess I had passed the test. A week or so later one of the trainers asked me if I wanted to fight in Lumpinee in a couple weeks. To them it was just another fight, but for me, it was the dream fight of my life.

The stadium is legendary, especially the original location. It was opened way back in 1956 and is run by the Thai military. Belts from the stadium were some of the most prestigious in the world and many legends like Samart Payakaroon, Hippy Sangmanee, Sagat Petchyindee, Dieselnoi Chor Thanasukarn, Jongsanan Fairtex and others had fought there. It was the mecca for Muay Thai.

I had only two pro fights and was in shock that I could get an amazing opportunity so soon in my career.

"You fight farang from Jitti Gym. 73kg," my trainer said to me.

At that time, I was weighing 173 pounds and needed to be 160.7 (73kg) but that didn't matter, I would fight at any weight just to fight at Lumpinee. I was in the best shape of my life. Doing the grind everyday got me tip top.

In the lead up to the fight they would set the round timer to four minute rounds and start every round with 10 kicks right and 10 kicks left. When the round was over you would do 10 pushups.

In the corners were a tarp like covering sewed into the ring so that the boxers could run water over their head to cool down and not get all over the canvas. These things separated the recreational training from the professional training.

Most of the bigger fights in Thailand have same day weigh-ins, something I wasn't accustomed to. I had the fight in Chaiyaphum and one fight without weigh-ins in Pattaya. I arrived at Lumpinee at six in the morning of the fight for the eight o'clock weigh-ins, just to make sure I was on weight. I stepped on the test scale and weighed exactly 160.7 lbs. I was pretty worn down and couldn't wait to refuel my body.

The promoter then walked up to my trainer and told him that the foreigner that I was supposed to fight had to pull out of the fight, but they had a replacement for me. He then told me that a more experienced Thai would fight in his place, but I needed to lose more weight if I wanted to fight him. I was worn from the weight cut but there was no way I was missing this opportunity to fight in Lumpinee where all my heroes had fought. I threw on the sauna suit and ran around the stadium for around 45 minutes to get the weight off.

Up and down the empty parking lot I went. My joints ached as I ran around the worn asphalt of the lot. I went into the sauna to try to sweat it out in there after a while. Broken tiles barely covered the dirt floor. The sauna looked to be in an abandoned area of the old stadium. The sweat was finally beginning to break

I finally got down to about 158 pounds and my opponent was 155.

"Okay, everything good," the promoter said.

After getting the extra weight off I had a nice Thai meal right there at the stadium. They had a huge tray of rice and a bunch of minced pork. I sat down with all the fighters, camps, coaches, and eating amongst everyone. I was the only foreigner fighting.

When I returned to home camp I was tired and went straight away to bed. I didn't have much time to rest and recover. At that time Lumpinee had an afternoon show for the up and comers and a night show for the more experienced. I was on the afternoon show. I couldn't fall asleep; my body was so tired from the cut. I started thinking, and thinking and thinking then all of a sudden there was a knock on the door to head to the stadium.

After sitting around at the stadium for a bit I started getting my fight trunks out, right as one of the Lumpinee officials walked by.

"You can not wear," he said, pointing at my shorts.

The trunks I brought couldn't be worn in the show because it had a brand on it that wasn't one of the sponsors of the show. He then asked me where my *prajiats* and anklets are for examination. I told him I don't fight with anklets.

I usually don't fight with *prajiats* too.

Prajiats are a part of the Muay Thai fighter's costume, especially in Thailand. Made of cloth they usually have a piece of sentiment woven into them, a mother's hair, or maybe a piece of a father's scarf. They're supposed to bring luck to the fighter.

"You must wear," he said.

Most of the time in these situations I tell inspectors to get lost but this was Lumpinee. So I went outside the stadium to the Twins store and bought the only anklets that would fit, pink ones. The store didn't have any arm bands.

"We make *prajiat* with tape," my trainers told me.

At that point I was wearing used promotion's trunks and pink anklets. The shorts were faded as hell and were a really off red.

Then my hands got wrapped.

In Thailand when it comes to wrapping hands anything goes. Very little gauze is used in a Thai wrap. You can roll tape and stack them on top of your knuckles. It's essentially a cast. None of the wraps I had done in Thailand would pass any USA sanctioning body. I thought that maybe in the big stadiums Lumpinee, Rajadamnern the inspector would come back around and sign off. Not the case. I got a nice hard taped cast.

I was massaged with *namman muay* and vaseline. The orange menthol substance heated my body and loosened me up. The vaseline was slathered on me to make blows slide off. My gloves were laced up. My *mongkol* was put on. I went up to the ring. As I went over the top ropes something came over me for just a quick second as my feet touched the canvas. I had made it. This was my dream as a fighter to be in the very ring that I saw Saenchai fight in just 2 years prior.

It was time to focus.

The bell rang. The fight started. In the first round we

began feeling each other out. He landed some good kicks, and I landed some good punches.

By the second the feeling out process was over and we began throwing down. He landed some big leg kicks, and I answered with punching. I connected with a straight right that scored a flash knockdown, but he was right back up with no count.

If you get up quick in Thailand, they won't give you a count but he was wobbled.

I then got right back on him, thinking I had him. I let everything go, but he answered back with a big elbow that split my forehead. The cut was right below the hairline. The blood poured down and I kept rubbing the blood off with my glove. It burned.

In the third he came out with more heavy leg kicks. I lifted to check one and it landed right on the soft spot of my knee cap that I had injured in Chaiyaphum. It flared up angry. I was checking only about half of the kicks thrown at me. I closed the distance and worked my knees and clinch. The adrenaline had taken over. I knew everything would be bad later but then, it was just about the fight.

As I began the clinch game, I ate another elbow on the forehead that opened up cut two. That one was right between my eyes.

Between the rounds, the trainers told me the cuts were pretty bad and asked if I wanted to keep going. Their faces were scrunched up with concern. They didn't want to look at the cut. It was all bad.

"That's no good," I thought. I had never felt more pain than in that fight. I couldn't stop.

My leg was destroyed. I was cut badly, twice.

There was no way I was quitting in Lumpinee. Round four started. We traded kicks, he was landing the better shots. I landed a hail mary spinning back elbow that rocked him. The crowd got wild. I tried to follow it up with knees to no avail. In the final seconds the Thai landed a few more heavy shots to my lead leg.

I was cut open and down on the cards. I went out throwing some big punches. Nothing landed clean. I ate a couple more leg kicks. I had to change to southpaw. We exchanged a couple more times. The fight was over.

I lost the fight, but it was entertaining at least. Of the eight fights that night my fight was the only one that went the distance. As I was leaving people were looking at me with their mouths wide open.

"Michael, many cut. *Mai dee*," my trainer said. He shook his head.

I looked in the mirror. I was carved pretty good.

I went to see the doctors. They cleaned up my cuts and stitched me up right there. Half an hour later I had fourteen stitches.

"Come back next week," the doctor said. He wanted to make sure everything healed up.

After the doctor I headed over to accounting to pick up my purse for the fight. I knew Saturday fighters didn't make as much as Tuesday and Friday night fighters but I was interested to see how much I was going to make. My trainer handed me 3,500 baht. It was awful, the equivalent of about $100 dollars US. I was hoping for 5,000 or 6,000 baht but they told me the crowds had been light lately because of the political crisis in Bangkok.

It wasn't about money. It was about stepping into the ring and stadium that legends have fought in. I gave half my money to the trainers for helping me out cornering and headed home.

I ended up at Foodland, Thailand's Denny's, with friends. I couldn't walk. I had to be carried to the cab to get there. When I arrived at the diner I felt some serious pain in my forehead. I painfully limped to the bathroom and took off the bandages and I looked at my stitches they had given me at Lumpinee. They were hideous. I looked like Frankenstein. I had train tracks across my head. My forehead was tied together with shoe strings.

I walked out of the bathroom and told the gang I needed to go to the hospital and get the stitches redone. I headed to the Bangna hospital. I got into the emergency room and the doctor stared at my forehead.

"Who did this stitching," he asked. "Who did this stitching? This is going to leave some bad scars. We can do over."

When it was all said and done I looked 10 times better, and I felt about 20 times better. My purse was totally gone. I had to come out of the pocket to fix up the mad Lumpinee doctor's stitch work. My knee was blown and my leg looked like it had a watermelon inside of it. All in all, I wouldn't take it back for anything.

Years later I saw in an article in Siam Fight magazine. They did a story on a gym in Bangkok. I saw one of the head trainers and it was the guy I fought, Chatchai Sor Kanitsorn. The article praised him for his fighting ability and stated his record was 120 wins out of 160 fights. I did pretty good for having two pro fights in Thailand.

The day after the fight I was pretty worthless. All the staff was off.

It was on Sunday so the trainers were all relaxing. I woke up for breakfast with the rest of the camp. I could barely get around so I hobbled over to my office to grab some ibuprofen. The trainers were getting on with their drinking a little bit earlier than normal so I hobbled across the street and had a few Leo Beers with them.

"Good job, you have good heart," they told me.

Having a good heart means everything. I felt pretty good but that was all going to change come Monday morning.

Every Monday morning, Mr. Wong, would have all of the Fairtex Bangplee camp come and give him a report in his office there. To say it was intimidating was an understatement. At these meetings he would speak to the Thai employees and sometimes he would have to raise his voice.

A stylish old patriarch, Mr. Wong had a voice that made men shiver and he used it often. The meanest of trainers would squirm like kids in grade school when he yelled.

Hearing it in Thai sounded worse than English for some reason. He had a large booming voice and an old school air to him. Then it would come to me.

"How are the camp numbers? How many students do we have," he would ask.

That day he looked at me. I had a million stitches across my face. My leg was beat. I was a mess.

"Michael, they tell me you lose your fight," he said.

"Yes sir. They ended up switching the opponent at weigh ins," I replied.

"But Michael you outweigh him by three pounds."

"Yes sir, but he was really skilled," I said.

"Michael, that guy don't fight in the stadiums anymore, and you can't beat him? He's old."

He shook his head and that was the end of that meeting and the end of Mr. Wong lining up any fights for me. One shot.

7

WMC SUPER 8

It took awhile to get back to training after the five rounds at Lumpinee. I was going to the local Thai massage to get herbal heat presses on my leg every day. Getting something done back home would be expensive.

Each session was only five dollars though. My leg was dark and swollen for two weeks.

The stitches came out but left some serious scarring. There was a pink slash right between the eyes. Another cut was below my hairline on the right side.

I had a total of 22 stitches after the repair.

I wasn't the type to sit around too long so I did half ass boxing for a little bit. I couldn't run, jump rope, or kick. Finally, after three weeks I was back to training full on. Then I got a call from Fairtex Pattaya manager Ted Okuno.

Ted was a Hawaiian Japanese guy that had been at Fairtex Pattaya for a few years. He knew the ropes of being a foreign camp manager, and being in Pattaya he had seen everything. Anytime I had a problem with trainers, trainer's wives, or any employees Ted would always give me advice. I was very grateful for his friendship and guidance. I had meltdowns two or three times and contemplated going back home but Ted always cooled me down.

"The World Muay Thai Council is coming to Pattaya to do a super eight one day tournament," he said. "They'll have two World Titles all on ESPN and Channel 9 Thailand.

"Cool. I'll get a van together with some of the Fairtex Bangplee students to come out and watch," I said.

"Yea bro have them come down to watch you fight," he said. "You're going to be in the 8-man tournament."

There was a pause in the conversation and then he picked things back up.

"How many fights have you had here in Thailand?"

"Four."

"Okay," he said shocked. "We're going to tell them you've had 20. You're tough. This will be good exposure for you."

I already had a fight lined up two weeks from the Pattaya show in Pathum Thani (just outside Bangkok). It was Muay Thai legend Sangtiennoi's show and was going to have

Somluck, Samart, and other legends in attendance. All of these guys are regarded as all-time greats. I wanted a chance to fight in front of them and maybe get noticed. I wanted to make sure I made it.

But this was my chance to get my foot in the door in International competition with the WMC bout. I needed to make both of these happen.

Training was the usual, running and conditioning in the morning and for the afternoon pads, bags, and core work. A week out, the equipment manager, Chano, told me they were going to do some videoing of the training and send the video guy out with me to the tournament to document everything.

"We're going to send a video guy with you to the Sangti-ennoi fight," he told me.

Chano had been with the company for ages. He's always liked the sport and is real business like. He's quiet and wears glasses, he'd be hard to pick out in a crowd but he's one of the main people responsible for the equipment side at Fairtex.

I arranged for Fairtex to take a van of students out for the fight day, with the camera people, and Neung. I always liked Neung, he was a meticulous trainer but the other trainers didn't like him much because he wasn't a good fighter. He really liked soccer and was tall for a Thai which made him really good for pad holding for the foreigners.

Neung was a hard worker around camp. He was always up sweeping before training started early in the morning. He had his father's face, but not the natural talent. He made up for it with his work ethic.

I got out a day early and stayed in the Fairtex tower at the resort. The "tower" was a little room Ted made at the resort when he was too tired to go home. It was in the back where they did laundry.

I took the bus alone out there and was pretty much on weight.

When I arrived a bunch of fighters were all in the sauna cutting some pounds. The weigh-ins were held at Fairtex Pattaya, in the north part of the beach side city. It was the nicest camp in Thailand at the time and had four rings, a big nice pool, and some tennis courts. There were all sorts of people milling about during the weight cut and IFMA General Secretary Stephan Fox was there as well. He's always been a go getter which you could see right away in his short but wiry frame.

"It's good to see an American in the mix," Fox said. "I remember you from the IFMA in 2008 and 2009. This will be a qualifying tournament for The Challenger Muay Thai Reality Show."

The Challenger was like The Contender 2 for Muay Thai but there was some sort of dispute with the naming so they continued on with a different name. He said whoever won the tournament tomorrow would win a Challenger WMC belt and is on the program. The winner of the show would get $100,000 US.

Ted told me of a cool Italian spot, because I had to go get my lucky spaghetti for my night before dish. The place was empty but the food was solid, great bread, good pasta, and good salad. It was one of those times where everything seemed to be working out.

The show was at Thepprasit Stadium in Pattaya in the southern part of the city. It was maybe a fifteen minute drive down there and there wasn't much to the place.

You hear the word stadium and you think rafters, arena, big crowds. That wasn't the case at Thepprasit. It was a metal roof covering with open air on the sides. The seats were just 10 rows of bleachers. Ringside was a few rows of small plastic chairs. If you were a foreigner living in Bangkok during these times it was the place where they could get matched. Lots of foreigner versus Thai matches were held there. Whenever I had students visiting for extended periods at Fairtex we would have to take them out there to get matched. No foreigner was ready for the Bangkok level of Muay Thai during my stay at Bangplee. We had a couple we put into the old Lumpinee but they had to prove themselves at Thepprasit first.

I weighed in and saw all the other fighters in the tournament. There were some solid resident foreigners; Antoine Pinto, Jason Woodham, and a really tough Koh Samui circuit Thai that had been cleaning up the scene on the island. I was excited. I checked out the flyer and it had my name as Corley Fairtex from the USA.

In Thailand, fighters have a fight name and the last name is usually the gym they train at or a sponsor. For instance, Yodsanklai Fairtex or Sittichai Sitsongpeenong, both of them carry their gym name. For a foreigner at that time to carry a gym name means you've been at it, and you earned it. I didn't think I was at that level to be carrying such a prestigious name as Fairtex. I didn't let it get to me too much until Ted came over with a coconut and told me Mr. Wong would be at the fights alongside all the big bosses of Muay Thai. The founder of Fairtex who was also a big time Lumpinee promoter was coming to the fights with some kid from Texas carrying the Fairtex name on a fight program going on Thai TV and ESPN Star. All I kept thinking about was our last talk after my loss at Lumpinee. He was disappointed.

I went in the back to get my hands wrapped by my trainer Neung. Neung was always calm before fights.

He would always check with "Micun ok?"

Then they called us all to an elevated walkway to the ring they constructed. They had all of us line up in our *mongkols* and flags because they were going to draw in the ring for the matches. As we were walking up they told us it was a fake draw and that they already got the matches set. I was to be taking on Jason Woodham from England who had been living and fighting out of the WMC Gym Lamai in Koh Samui for a couple years at that time. He had around 50-60 fights. Woodham used to go by the moniker of "The Handsome Hero." He was a thin Brit and a really funny talker. He would fluctuate in weight.

He was game. He would take fights from 68 kg to 73 kg.

After the president of IFMA Dr. Sackchye had a speech in the ring, we were up.

"This is a true stepping stone for Muay Thai," the president said.

Ted came by and gave me some very detailed advice. "Fuck 'em up bro," he said.

I bumped gloves with him and saw Shuki, an older foreign fighter in Thailand who had made a name for himself fighting top Khmer fighters and being very tough. He told me to put the pressure on from the start and I could stop Jason.

Shuki was the most unassuming fighter you would see in Thailand, tall and skinny, older looking, but the guy was tough and could fight. Some of my favorite trainers from Fairtex Pattaya also came and stood in my corner, Ram, Rambo, Seesom, all those guys were there. The trainers at Bangplee had to listen to me, but the Pattaya ones didn't and they were always much nicer and welcoming. Having them there lifted me up. I felt good.

The fight opened up and we just went at it back and forth landing everything. Both of us were not really blocking anything but it was technical. As the round ended I wasn't tired and we both had a crazy pace going. I never told Woodham but he hit me with a clean knee to the body that I hid really well. I bounced out and moved around for a second to get my breath back. Overall I took the round.

Round two started.

"Go! Go! Go," I could hear all the Fairtex trainers, Shuki, Ted, the Fairtex students all yelling at me.

I never heard the crowd when I was fighting but I heard them in this fight, and I did just that, I just kept coming forward. I tried some stupid flying elbow and I was off balance afterward. I was against the ropes for the first time in the fight and when he came near I clinched and landed a flush knee to the body that bent him over. It left me with an opening for my favorite punch, the uppercut. It dropped him. I ran over to the neutral corner and knew I had it. If he got up from that he would still be on wobbly legs.

To his credit he got up, Jason was one tough fighter, all of his fights were exciting. He came right at me but I was still hype from getting him down and I unloaded punches on him against the ropes and I pulled his head down and kneed him flush on the face and he was done.

I've never celebrated a victory but some reason I did some shimmy thing after I got the KO.

I didn't know what the fuck I was doing; I can't dance for shit. I was just pumped. I saw on the VIP stage all the Thai bosses applauding and I saw Mr. Wong smile and give me sort of a nod and he clapped as I *wai'd* to him. I don't think I ever made that guy proud while working for him but maybe for just a moment he was that day.

I got out of the ring and I got to the back and Ted got me a coconut.

"Good job bro," he said. "You fucked him up."

I chuckled a bit. I stood around watching the other fights and felt a lot of pain in my lead leg. My lead leg, the one where I broke my patella in my first pro fight and the one that got trashed in Lumpinee. I didn't want to show it, so I sat down.

Antoine Pinto had just fought a week before in the Queen's Cup and where he lost a decision to Saiyok. For this show his first opponent was from Brazil and he got rid of him quick.

The Thai followed up and TKO'd his opponent as well. A well known Malaysian Faizal Ramli stopped his opponent from Turkey and was my next opponent.

The second fight came up and my strategy was to go big early because I didn't think my leg would hold up. The fight opened and I worked some nice jabs and threw up a quick head kick he blocked. I then throw my favorite uppercut set up, a slight over hand right, and then come right back with an uppercut. I landed both big. As I rushed to capitalize he threw an inside kick that tripped me up. I thought nothing of it and got up then my leg went out.

"Shit," I thought.

I started the fight strong and knew he had nothing for my boxing but my leg was gone and he knew it. He came at me so hard after that just continually going after my leg. I got offset again and stumbled getting back up. The ref was getting real close to me and I knew it was about that time. Faizal landed another good kick and I was bouncing on one leg and the ref called it. I didn't want to go out like that.

I got some help going to the back and surprisingly everyone told me how much they enjoyed watching me. The trainers were happy, and having all the Fairtex students come around for photos was cool too.

"How much longer are you going to be in Thailand," Stephan Fox said. He'd come up to me after all the fans had cleared off. "The show needs an American. Keep after it and maybe we'll have another qualifier."

That gave me something to be hopeful about even though my leg was a mess.

I got to see Jason too. We talked about how we just went crazy in there. We met by the medical area where everyone was getting stitched up. He was still a bit cloudy from the uppercut that got him.

"How many fights have you had," he asked.

"Now, six or seven."

"What the hell? Just seven?"

"Well our system is different in America. I had 15 amateur bouts in Muay Thai and 11 amateur boxing fights."

We talked about living and fighting in Thailand as we watched the Thai take out Antoine. Antoine was solid but took too much damage in Queens cup the week prior. Then Faizal, who I fought, was even with the Thai in the finals but the Thai's shoulder came out of socket and he ate some elbows from not defending himself well. The ref decided to wave it off.

Seeing that I could hang with guys gave me motivation. I rode back in the Fairtex van with the students. The whole trip I was on a high. I'd fought on Thai TV for the first time, made Mr. Wong happy for just a second, and got my foot in the door with WMC.

Usually after a fight I'd go drink with the trainers or the students, but my knee was messed up and I was supposed to be fighting on Sangtiennoi's big show in Pathum Thani in two weeks. I went back to the massage by the gym and had them get out the herbal heat press and start on my leg again. The shop was an old massage place connected to a gas station. They would treat me with an herbal press for 350 baht. The masseuses would always laugh and joke about me coming in there all beat up all the time.

Knowing I couldn't run I started riding the bike each

morning. For the whole week I didn't do any Muay Thai just rode a stationary bike and got herbal presses/massages.

A lady who used to work in the office at Fairtex was doing guest relations at another camp in Bangkok reached out to me for the fight. She told me it was day before weigh-ins at 12pm and that I would be fighting a Thai. I took an hour-long taxi out to Pathum Thani only to find that the weigh-ins weren't till 3pm. They did a press conference for it too. I didn't know anything.

It was when Thai Fight was just starting up. Thai Fight was a show on TV that put high level Thai's against foreigners in tournaments. From what I was told this show was some sort of duplicate with the backing of Sangtiennoi, Somluck, and Samart.

At the press conference I had no idea who I was fighting. I saw a bunch of recognizable faces but didn't know anything. I weighed in and headed back to Fairtex.

The next day Chano told me to take the video guy with me and Neung. We headed out and started getting ready for the fights. It was a nice set up. They had nice lights, TV cameras, and smoke machines. It was really rare for a Thai show at the time. I did my normal warm up. I stretched really well and shadow boxed. I tried to visualize myself in the ring and what would happen. Then they called me to get ready.

We were in the back and they had me and my Thai opponent who I just saw sit down next to each other. He was short with big legs and had a bunch of *sak yant* on his back. They called him in and it was a fancy walk out. It was all new to me in Thailand. I was thinking this may be bigger than I thought. It was perfect timing too, me with a bummed leg. They called me in and it was go time.

For the first and only time I switched stances throughout the fight to not show my leg was damaged. I landed body kicks, and for the first time fought smart. Problem was, while

I was keeping my lead leg from taking damage, I was eating a ton of teeps and really good ones. It was just a three round fight but it was close each round. In the final round with ten seconds left I threw a jumping spike elbow that got the crowd all riled up. It wasn't enough, and I lost the decision. I was happy to not take further damage but wanted to open up a little more. It was more of a technical bout, and in all of my previous bouts I never did that. I learned a lot from it.

To put it simple I got outclassed on points. I did some really good stuff but he made me look stupid. I got off balanced with teeps. He would always end the clinch in a better position. All the little points that make a fighter look better, he did them.

Thinking it wasn't going to be received well by the crowd, I had a lot of Thai and foreigners tell me good fight. So I sat in the crowd and watched some of the fights and the lady that got me the fight came by with an envelope of money. She mentioned that she had to take her percentage and this was what I got afterward. It was 1500 baht, about $50 USD. I was like what the hell?

"It costs 800 baht to drive out here," I told her.

There and back I had to come out of pocket.

I always tipped my trainer for fights so I had to come out of pocket for that too. I gave them 600 baht or so.

Have you ever lost money fighting? I did. It was the close of a rough three weeks, but experience you can't get anywhere else in the world.

When I was in the car on the way back they told me my opponent used to be pretty solid and had around 150 fights but didn't fight in the stadiums anymore.

8

HOLIDAY IN CAMBODIA

I got the message about fighting in Cambodia after fighting the WMC 8-Man tournament in Pattaya. Knowing that it was a neighboring country of Thailand, I knew it wasn't a big paying fight but it was a new country I hadn't fought in and Cambodia had some tough Khmer fighters.

As I was training for the fight a friend sent me a newspaper clip from Cambodia that had me and the other seven fighters on there. My bout was an eight-man tournament featuring four Cambodian fighters and four foreign fighters. The tournament was for Cambodia's gold belt and it was sponsored by one of Cambodia's top whiskeys, Gold Regent. It was a pretty big deal and featured the top Khmer fighters.

I was in. I hadn't won a legitimate belt as a professional and I was hungry.

The pay in Cambodia wasn't bad, it was about $1200 and was actually higher than any of the fights I had previously in Thailand. After making several visa runs by bus to Cambodia, first starting out as an employee of Fairtex, I was happy to hear that we were being flown over for the fight.

I put in a decent two weeks of training and made my way to the airport. I saw a familiar face, a former Fairtex sponsored fighter, Scottish Champion Stephen Meikle. He was about my height and was in good shape. He had a good clinch game style. On my first trip to Thailand in 2008 I met him at the Fairtex Bangplee camp that I managed. We've always kept up with each other's fights.

We were both looking for the manager Sasan, manager of Buakaw and owner of Super Export Shop, that booked us the fights. Sasan was a tall heavy weight, a former Persian fighter. His fighting days were long past him but he still towered over people. He was hard to miss. And he wasn't there.

He then called me about an hour before the flight and said he wasn't going to make it and that former champion Shuki from Israel was going to be meeting us in Cambodia to assist with cornering and management. Shuki was the long-time resident fighter and coach living in Thailand that was at the WMC Super 8 show.

It was both our first time in Phnom Penh, Cambodia and didn't know what hotel we were staying at, how to get around, nothing.

We arrived in Phnom Penh and the airport was empty. We headed over to the Visa station and they made us purchase some "special" visa. It seemed like some shakedown thing for tourists. We just stood around and began to realize we were the only two foreigners in the airport. It was good and bad news. The good was that if there is a driver, he would be able to spot us easily. The bad news was that no one else was there.

A man approached us and raised his hand in a fight stance.

"Boxers!?"

"Yes," I replied.

He took us outside to a van, drove 30 minutes into town and put us at a hotel which was very, very sketchy. Both of us had to share a room that was overlooking a trash site. Children were scavenging over the rubble looking for food, it was very heartbreaking and depressing to see it.

"How's your weight," I asked Stephen after we'd settled in. We had weigh-ins at 8am the next day and fights in the late afternoon on TV. Both he and I were over by about five pounds or two kilos.

We ran down to the lobby and asked the front desk if there were saunas around.

"Yes, many," the receptionist said. "Taxi."

We jumped in a cab.

"Sauna," I said.

The driver smiled.

"Ok. No problem," he replied.

At the sauna they charged us two US dollars. We got some keys and headed to the locker room. We disrobed and grabbed a towel and headed to the sauna room.

It was maybe five minutes in the sauna before two girls came in with buckets of salt. The girls had on short shorts and loose fitting shirts. When I saw them I knew something was going on.

We waved no.

"Lose weight for boxing. Just sweat," we said.

The two of them looked at each other puzzled and then left. A few minutes later, a man came in and asked us to leave the sauna. We were mad. It was the night before the fight and we are getting worked over by the spa. Not the right type of sauna.

Another cab driver took us to another spot and the same thing happened.

"How many girls you want to sit with," the host said.

"No! We are not interested in any females in the sauna with us."

At this one, we didn't even go into the locker room, we just left. The cab driver took us to what finally looked like a normal sauna. It seemed legit. In the lobby were a bunch of old Chinese men coming in after work. It was a really good sauna. They had a really hot, dry sauna and also had a cold pool, but it must've been one o'clock in the morning the day of the fight before we had finished up.

We made our way back home and I tried to lay down, but I couldn't sleep and got up at 3am. I woke up to irregular heartbeats and palpitations. It was the first time cutting weight made me feel like that. I felt like I was about to go into some sort of shock. I was paranoid. I couldn't sleep. I got up and drank a little bit of water, but that got my mind racing knowing that it would put on the weight. That didn't help with sleep either.

"Man I gotta eat something but what can I eat," I asked Stephen.

He suggested I eat just a little rice soup. It helped ease my mind a little.

I don't ever remember what time I actually laid down, but when I woke up at 7am that morning, I felt like I hadn't had any sleep at all.

We were both out the door before 7:15am, because in Cambodia, like Thailand it was same day weigh-in. When we got to the stadium a lot of the Cambodians stared and pointed at us, laughing. We stepped on the scales. We were both heavy by several kilos.

"You better make weight, you better make weight or you don't get paid," the promoter yelled.

We stepped aside to watch the Cambodians weigh-in. The Cambodians also weighed in heavy, so the Cambodians looked at us with a blank stare. We looked at them with a blank stare. A mutual agreement between us was made that something was off with the scale without both sides saying a word. The Khmer fighters and us the foreigners looked at the promoter with our hands up like, "Hey man this scale is off and both sides agree," but the promoter was not having it.

He was a short angry looking man that had obviously fought before. Scars lined his face and he had that old boxer style to him.

Stephen and I put on some sauna suits and started running a track that was at the weigh ins. It was like a college facility and the track I imagine was standard Olympic length but wasn't paved. It was just a dirt track. I must have jogged a little over a mile and walked another mile. I just didn't have the energy to run anymore. I walked over to the scale and I finally made weight. It was 10am the day of the fight, and the fight was at 3pm on Cambodian TV. I only had a couple hours to refuel my body. Stephen still had just a little bit to get off before I left.

A taxi driver took me to the town square area and found a Cambodian equivalent of Pizza Hut. I got some spaghetti and meat sauce with some bread. It was my traditional meal before a fight and it was terrible. There was no grocery, and no help to get properly refueled. I couldn't have a proper meal. There were no electrolyte drinks, water, chicken and vegetables. I had maybe an hour nap back at the hotel and got the call, it was time to head over to the stadium.

We arrived back at the stadium at 2pm for the 3pm fights. I found out that I was fighting the Cambodian champion who had over 130 fights. Stephen and I got to the locker rooms and when I say locker rooms I use that term loosely. It was a brick building with no plumbing. It was simply brick wall stall barriers and brick squares that were the toilet. The grossest bathrooms I've ever been in my life. I nervously sat in the back, not feeling really well from the weight cut still groggy from the bad food and lack of sleep.

There was an un-televised undercard that was going on as we were sitting around in the back. There was only going to be four bouts that day and I was the last one. The first two fights went fast and all of a sudden Stephen was up. This happens a lot in Asia, because they don't fill time if the fights go fast. I started shadow boxing to get loose.

I watched Stephen's bout on a small beat to hell TV in the back while I tried to warm up. The stadium was really small and I would peek through the curtains to watch the action live.

"I lost. I got robbed," Stephen said angrily.

I thought it was a close fight. He did good but it wasn't anything to get mad about. When you're not the hometown guy you're not going to get the nod on a close decision in Cambodia of all places.

It was my time to go out. In Cambodia you walk to the ring with just your hand wraps and they put the gloves on in the ring. As I walked to the ring I noticed that everyone in the crowd was Cambodian. Everyone pointed at me and looked at me as if I was going to get sacrificed. It was the first time in my fight career that I questioned what the fuck was I doing here fighting in Cambodia. In Muay Thai it is always traditional to go over the ropes and when I jumped over the ropes my legs nearly gave out upon landing. I was still not hydrated and my legs were still cooked from all the running to get the weight off. What the hell was I thinking?

The announcer called out my name and they put the gloves on me. I raised my hand to acknowledge the crowd but was treated with silence. The Cambodian champion was announced with a record of 125 wins and 15 losses.

"Thun Sophea," the announcer cried.

The crowd erupted with cheers.

It had been so dead when I went out. The announcers, the fans, everyone was there for him. They wanted to see me get destroyed.

The bell rang and round one was a feeling out process, but I didn't feel good. Everything he touched with me to the head hurt. The weight cut definitely took its toll on my body and at the end of the first round I threw an overhand right variation that hit right off the Cambodian's head breaking my thumb. My go to, my best weapon, the right hand, was taken away. I went to the corner at the end of the first round and told my corner I broke my thumb, but there wasn't not much he could do and he just told me to keep on fighting.

The second round started and I started getting my inside leg hacked up. He was a southpaw and his power rear kick was landing nicely on my lead inside leg. Shortly after he landed a flush but not hard punch that dropped me. I couldn't take any headshots. The weight cut had my brain dried out. I got up still out of it. Two more knockdowns and the referee thankfully stopped the fight.

It was the second worst fight in my life. It was recorded live on Cambodian TV and hours later was global on YouTube. I went back to the prison-like locker room to get my stuff.

I went to my opponent's locker room and congratulated him and looked for a doctor. I could barely get my hand wraps off due to pain. The doctor looked over my hand.

"I think it is broken," he said. "When you go to Thailand you fix."

Stephen and I gathered our things and went back to the hotel angrily, both of us upset with our performance. We went and grabbed a bite to eat and a couple beers.

"Hey guys you had a bad night, *mai pen rai*, don't worry, that's Muay Thai, you come back and you fight again," our coach Shuki said. He patted us on the shoulder and shrugged.

I wanted to fight again to erase this horrible experience.

We had a flight the next morning but Stephen and I wandered Phnom Penh. The city has got to be one of the craziest places I've ever been in my life. We made our way through the streets and random people offered us bags of drugs and women. Then one man came up to us.

"Do you wanna shoot guns," he asked. "You can shoot at cow."

He pointed at all these high powered weapons.

We went up to a pub and grabbed a couple beers. Inside the pub people were just casually smoking weed. You could find joints just sitting around on the bar tops. The place was empty so after those two beers we went back out in the streets and started asking some of the tuk tuk drivers where the place was to be. It was a bad idea just like it is in Thailand. They wanted to take you to all the tourist trap spots where they get a commission. We went to an Internet café to look up places to go in Phnom Penh. We found out that the best place to be was on the river that flew through the city. When we got near the river we started seeing other tourists and backpackers. A lot of people were drunk and crazy so we didn't stick around long. A lot of the backpackers were the typical wanna-be smelly junky hippies from Khaosan road in Bangkok and didn't have much to add to the conversation. Stephen and I had spent a lot of time in Bangkok and were used to a little more action.

We got in a cab. He took us to one of those tourist trap bars where you walk in, you just know it's sketchy. The people inside this bar were some of the grossest looking people I've ever seen in my life. They were the sex tourist rejects of Thailand. They were the men that Thailand wouldn't take, the worst of the worst. There were several Europeans with one eye bigger than the other. They had the scariest outfits, in the weirdest stares you've ever seen. They wore old tropical Hawaiian shirts with the buttons not fully done. Their pregnant bellies stuck out and they wore sandals exposing their gross feet to the world.

Every woman that was in the place was a working girl and kept walking up to me and Stephen propositioning us. We were only in for 10 minutes and knew that we needed to get out of there.

"These are sex mutants...the worst," Stephen said as we left.

I couldn't stop laughing.

As we were walking out the door, a couple motorcycle taxis made some comments. They were pointing and laughing, dogging on our fights that were on tv earlier. We paid no attention.

Then a little Cambodian dwarf, who looked to be a door

guy asked us where we were going next. It was like a scene from Fear And Loathing In Las Vegas, but it was real prostitutes, small persons, and more nasty sex mutant tourists. It was the worst bar I'd ever been in, so we headed back towards the hotel area of town and dropped in on one last little bar area. Guys came up to us again offering to shoot guns.

"You can shoot cows. You can shoot livestock anything. No problem," they pointed at pictures of cows.

As we made our way home we got a few more cat calls from working women, and more drug offers.

"Fuck all this," I said.

We got back to bed and I stared out my window; once more and saw the children, families, digging through the trash and really felt bad for this country I was in.

A Cambodian by the name Thy Bun Rith (Racky) messaged me after my fight and told me that several students liked seeing someone from America fight on TV there. He did outreach work for the underprivileged in Cambodia. His group was the CAD Children's Action for Development.

"How can I help," I asked him.

After being in that country and seeing it firsthand, I sent over $150 immediately. He shot some photos of what I got the kids. It was great.

It's always a pain to get money transferred there. You have to go through so much just to get a transfer over and then the fees are bad too. Cambodia still doesn't have PayPal or Facebook money.

I keep in touch still. In 2019 I brought equipment to them.

Cambodia will always be in my mind, not just because of the sights and the kids but because of the whole fight experience, me on TV all pale and sickly and how bad I was. I know that I weighed in, just hours before the fight against Cambodia's number one fighter.

When I was back home in Bangplee I phoned my parents. My mom picked up.

"What happened? What went wrong?"

"Everything."

I could hear my dad rustling around in the background yelling for my mom to give him the phone. Definitely a few beers in.

"What the hell was that?! I saw it on YouTube, you looked like you hadn't been outside in days. What bar did they drag you out of to go fight this guy," I could hear him yelling in the background.

He was right, I told him the whole story, but he was right. I did look awful.

But it wasn't over just yet. After a day of resting at the camp I went to Bangna hospital to get X-Rayed. Just below my thumb, was a fracture. The doctor suggested a surgery or warned I wouldn't be able to have good motion in my thumb again. I opted out because I was a broke foreigner working on Thai wages in Thailand. I even opted out of getting a full cast. They made a mold that started mid thumb and went up half the inside of the forearm and wrapped with standard wrap. This didn't allow for my thumb to move at all so I was good to go in my young dumb eyes.

When I was back at my office, one of the lobby girls told me Mr. Wong was there and wanted me back at the complex for our usual Monday meeting.

These meetings never went well as Fairtex Bangplee was on its downfall when I took over. We didn't even get into the bad numbers of the camp.

"What happened to your arm," he asked right away.

"I fought this weekend in Cambodia and lost."

"You lost in Cambodia, you break your arm," He shook

his head. "I don't know why you do this. You win some but you are not in top class in Thailand. So why do you do this? I think you need to stop this."

I tuned him out. I was taken aback by him telling me that I basically sucked. I knew I wasn't going to be fighting for a Lumpinee belt but I wanted to see just how far I could go. I wanted to keep growing and learning but at what cost and when was enough, enough?

9

TOYOTA CUP

D oing favors for promoters got me pretty banged up but also got me opportunities for big shows. After the Cambodia disaster Sasan asked me if I would be interested in fighting in the Toyota Cup Marathon. I was so excited for the opportunity, all the greats had fought in that tournament Saenchai, Nong 0, Yodsanklai, Petchboonchu, etc.

Only two Americans had ever fought in the tournament Kevin Ross, and Cyrus Washington. I remember sitting in the Fairtex lobby watching them compete in the tournament telling myself I had to get on there.

I was stoked. The tournament was a one-day 8 Man broadcast live on TV for the Toyota Belt, a big purse, and a new Toyota truck. It is pretty big stakes anywhere and especially in Thailand.

I needed to train as hard as I could for this 8-Man tournament because there were six international fighters and two Thais.

I had to carry out a lot of new rule changes passed on to me at the camp. Being a foreigner and head of Muay Thai camp, it didn't come off well to all of the trainers. They knew I had a fight coming up but they had no idea it was the Toyota Cup. Because of some of the new rules I had to carry out, all of them basically ignored me. They were "too tired" to train me. It was not good. Even my main trainer Neung was getting pressured from other trainers not to train me.

My biggest fight opportunity and I wasn't getting any pad work with any trainer. This only fueled me to get in my best shape possible. I got up early each morning and ran longer runs and in the afternoons, I would run again and just shadow box. My work got the attention of Muay Thai legend and Fighter Of The Century, Apidej Sit Hirun. Apidej was getting older and many times needed time away because he was ill but he always had a lot of spirit in his face.

He would approach me and *wai.*

"Man-ager," he would say to me. "Jogging then train with me."

Apidej was getting up there in age and wasn't able to hold much of pads but he insisted on working with me. A lot of the trainers would laugh at us working together but I didn't care. They helped me zero percent for that fight.

Apidej was about 5'10 and looked every bit that. He had around 300 fights. He kept sort of a buzzed cut with pepper black hair and kept a mole on his face unattended and hairy for good luck. His face just had the look of a man that had seen it all, but always carried a smile, and that smile really showed when we worked together.

Apidej would show me old school tricks that were no longer legal in Muay Thai. Every day leading up to that fight he would come talk to me while I was on the treadmill.

"Managerrrr! Jogging then train! Krap," he would say with a smile.

He kept my spirits high when I was feeling down. He would always make me smile and laugh during our sessions. I always told him he didn't have to call me manager. I even had the front desk girls translate it to him. I thought of him as a legend and he did not have to call me that. He would shake his head and laugh and in Thai say that I was the manager.

Two to three weeks out from the bout and I had to go to a press conference for the tournament. I had never done a full on press conference for a fight. When I got there I met up with some of the others in the tournament, Stephen Meikle, four other foreigners, and the two Thais (Petchmonkong Petchfocus, and Aikpracha Meenayotin).

In attendance was Rob Cox. I shook hands and met up with the legendary foreign authority on Muay Thai at the presser and right off the bat he inquired after me.

"How's camp coming along," the tall Englishman asked me in his west London accent.

"I'm on my way out," I replied. "The camp is losing money. They're making me change things. The trainers hate me for it. It's just not easy. There's a lot of competition."

More and more big camps were popping up in central Bangkok and attracted more tourists. My camp, Bangplee, was about 45 minutes outside of central Bangkok and there was not a thing to do out there. To make it worse, all of the famous fighters out of Fairtex were taken from the Bangplee camp over to the Pattaya camp.

I couldn't believe how much press there was. There had to be over 100 journalists, photographers etc. They called for all the fighters and had us get into fight trunks. Then we were called out to shadow box in front of all the press. Thai champion Aikpracha went first. I went next. I went out and smoke cannons popped and there was fog everywhere I just started to shadow like I'd done it before.

Lights flashed and cameras snapped as the smell of artificial smoke filled my nose. I punched the air and threw a long knee. It was one of those moments where I was in awe.

After all the fighters got up and took pictures a Thai man came up to me,

"Michael, I take you to fight in two weeks, meet at Lumpinee, ok," he said.

I had no idea who he was but he knew me.

"You need training, come to my gym, Muay Thai Plaza," he said.

Things were starting to click after the Rob Cox conversation and now this man appeared out of nowhere asking me to come train at his gym. I learned later that he was a freelancer with a hand in everything, the Toyota Cup, Thai Fight, Cambodia bouts... He was a wheeler and dealer and he was giving me something new. It was a sign. If I'm not getting any training and the trainers don't wanna work, I needed to leave Fairtex.

When I got back to camp I trained a couple days with Apidej, the other trainers still had no idea I was fighting for the Toyota Cup. I decided to go into the city and see what

Muay Thai Plaza was all about. The Thai man greeted me, I still didn't know his name. He was sincere and friendly then told me to warm up and that he would have a trainer ready for me. After some rounds of the usual, jump rope, shadow box, I got pointed to a trainer, no timer rounds. I just got dogged out. They worked me really good and then sent me in to clinch with some of the other foreign fighters and Thais. It was a great experience. One of the fighters from Iran I recognized from the past Toyota Cup, Vahid Roshani.

"Hey man, what's up," I said to him.

"I didn't know you work with Mr. Pong," Roshani replied.

"I was like yeah, I guess I just started."

I got back to the camp and was business as usual. Then during my own little strength and conditioning session, I incurred one of the worst injuries I have had in this sport. I had on light resistant bands and was shadowboxing knees. Upon lifting my knee, I felt this pulled muscle, tear feeling, on my right side of my groin and lower abdomen. It was so much pain that I went numb and just hit the ground and took off the bands.

I laid on my back and looked at the ceiling. I didn't know what was going on. I tried to get up and engage my core in a sit up like movement but I was in serious pain. I went to my room and took a painful shower, changed and got over to my work laptop to Google what just happened.

Upon some research I realized I had an inguinal hernia. I couldn't find a remedy in Thailand. I messaged my parents back home and told them I needed a hernia belt ASAP. It didn't matter the cost. I had to make this fight.

For the remaining two weeks of training for the fight I did not throw kicks at over 50% because the pivoting and lifting my leg hurt so much. My belt arrived five or so days later and it put pressure on the area of pain where I was at least able to do some very light kicks. It looked like a jockstrap but instead of a cup that goes over the junk there's a pad that goes on your stomach. The padding put pressure on abs. I wore it throughout the entire day even when I wasn't training.

The day before the fights we had to meet at a hospital near the big Siam Paragon mall for weight check. There was also a WBC Boxing World Title on the card there was a ton of press at the weight check. Having that hernia belt on really restricted me from the amount of running I wanted to do to get the last few pounds off.

There was a spa near Fairtex called Jittrawon that had a really good wet and dry sauna and cold pool. I used that to cut about eight pounds the day before and morning of weigh ins. I stepped on the scale and made weight the first try. I started to replenish with my favorite go to post weight check drink in Thailand Pocari Sweat. It's a lemon-lime Japanese electrolyte drink and is really good. It was watery but crisp.

As I was rehydrating Mr. Pong from Muay Thai Plaza came over to me. He had a long face, rough teeth, but an easy smile. He was always wearing western shirts. That day he wore a simple tee shirt with the Nike swoosh on it.

"You need ride tomorrow to Saraburi," he asked.

"Saraburi? Where's that? "

"That's where the fights are tomorrow, meet me at Lumpinee stadium. I drive you, eight o'clock," he said.

Before heading back to camp I decided to head over to the mall to get some post weigh -in food. I saw a familiar steak house that I'd seen in the States but had never been to, Tony Roma in Siam Paragon. I wanted something tried and true. I got a salad and a bunch of water.

I decided on a chicken breast with sides of vegetables and potatoes.

"Chicken no have," the waiter said.

I ordered a New York strip, something I had never eaten

post weigh in. It tasted pretty good but after two or three bites I knew it wasn't a good idea.

I took a taxi back to the camp and rested a bit. Some of the trainers caught on that I was fighting tomorrow and were pretty excited and startled to find out I was fighting in the Toyota Cup the following day. Because none of them helped with training and Apidej was too old and couldn't make the trip with me the next day I asked our newly hired MMA Coach Erik Gerber to come along.

Erik had been at the camp for three or four months. He'd had a few MMA fights before coming out and he'd just had his first Muay Thai fight. All the Thais thought we were related. We had the same blondish brown hair but he had cauliflower ears and I of course was better looking.

We had gotten to be pretty good friends out there in Thailand. After that was settled I went to Foodland and got my lucky night before dish, spaghetti. I always remembered growing up when my dad would run marathons or bike and he would eat spaghetti. My mom made a good one, so it always stuck with me. I woke up the next morning nice and early but noticed I hadn't gone #2 since weigh in. I peed multiple times but felt very bloated. I had some fresh fruit and vegetables for breakfast.

Eric and I took a taxi to Lumpinee Stadium to meet Mr. Pong. When we arrived at Lumpinee we just waited out front. No one was there and then from up above on the new second level, training facility trainer, Petch from Petchyindee Academy, waved at me.

He was such a nice guy and would always see me bringing tourists from Fairtex to Lumpinee to watch the fights. We actually worked together on a couple of projects for the Tourism Authority of Thailand. He was really excited to hear I was fighting in the Toyota Cup and he wished me luck.

Eventually I saw a beat to hell truck pull up and I figured

that was our ride. Mr. Pong and another guy got out and greeted Eric and I.

"Saraburi almost two hours, You go up front, Michael lay in the back of truck, relax," Mr. Pong said.

I laid in the back of the truck next to a spare tire and put my head on my backpack and tried to nap riding in the back of a truck for the two hours before I fought.

We arrived at Saraburi and it was a cool setup. They had a ring with a temporary cover over it and in the background of the ring was a small mountain. On the outskirts of the ring were Toyota trucks with huge banners with my picture on it alongside all the others. Mr. Pong told me that his trainer would help me with my hand wraps and cornering.

We set up our mat on the floor. Which in Muay Thai is like marking your territory, you lay your mat over a floor area and that is your setup for the fight. I laid down and rested for a bit but I still hadn't gone #2. I felt like a potbellied pig.

"I have to shit really bad," I told Eric. "I'm getting really worried."

"Get your trunks on," one of the organizers told everyone. "We draw for fight."

The nerves started to kick in and I could finally feel my stomach starting to move. All eight of the fighters walked into the ring. Everyone sized each other up. The TV cameras were rolling. Everyone went up and drew out of a hat.

I was hoping to meet Aikpracha in the final and not the first fight.

The spaghetti worked. My first draw was against an Australian kid that had been living and fighting out of Pattaya for a while. Everybody wai'd to each other and the camera then exited the ring.

"Get your gloves on," the organizer said. "You fight."

Finally, I felt I could go to the restroom and it was literally minutes before we were supposed to be ready to go by the ring. I stayed in there and made sure I got it all out sweating bullets. I got back and laid on my back to get the Thai oil put on. The trainer started to push my stomach down to my lower abdominal. They do this always before fights to push out everything and try to have you use the restroom before your fight so you are clear. I couldn't do this because the pushing down would make my hernia pain even worse.

"No. No. *Jep mak*," I told the trainer.

I finished with the oil. I was really debating on wearing the hernia belt during the fight but decided against it. I thought it would be cheating. I didn't know what the rules were.

The trainer tied on my steel cup up and then we walked toward the ring. They had all of us get into the ring and to save time they had all eight of us do our *wai kru*. All eight of us were just standing around in the ring.

"Now! Now! *Wai kru*," the TV guy yelled at us.

I went through my *wai kru* and I *wai*'d to the center of the ring. I looked around and me and only two other fighters were done. The others were still going. The camera kept panning around.

"Keep going. *Wai kru*," The TV guy yelled.

"What the hell," I muttered.

I went back to the center of the ring, hit my knees and wai'd three times.

"Ok. Ok. Good. Finish," they said at my second *wai*.

We all got out confused and sat around the ring.

I had no idea what bout I was but we were all sitting around the ring and they called in the French fighter World Champion Mikael Lallemoad and Contender Reality show fighter Zidov Akuma. The fight ended in less than a minute with Lallemand winning by TKO.

Next I saw another one round stoppage with Aikpracha brutally stopping his opponent. They called me and the fighter from Australia into the ring.

My strategy for one day tournaments was always the same, try and finish as fast as I could. The round started and he was very aggressive but his hands weren't sharp so I tried to capitalize early. I overthrew an overhand that was quite possibly the worst I've ever missed in a fight. I laughed a little after catching myself.

Midway through the first round he walked right into a jab, hook, cross, that rocked him badly and he took a couple steps back. I landed an uppercut as soon as his head rose. I smashed a huge cross that dropped him. It ended the fight. I was pumped to score a KO on Thai TV on such a big tournament.

I came out of the ring. Mr. Pong gave me a thumbs up and pointed me to sit back down. I was high on the fight and quickly sat down and watched my two potential opponents. Both stood over 6'2 and were 70kg. In the second round French-Algerian Yacine Darkrim stopped his opponent. There wasn't much break time. They told us that the semi-final fights would go right on without any break. If you got past the semi-final fight you would get a break, as that was where they had the WBC Boxing title fight on after.

Mr. Pong came over and gave me an orange soda in a bag with a straw.

"You need energy for next fight Michael," he said laughing.

I watched the first semifinal bout and saw Aikpracha walk through a high level fighter quite easily.

I was up. I was usually the bigger fighter at 70kg but not this time. The guy was close to 6'4. The bout opened with a couple hand exchanges and then I caught a kick and off balanced him with a sweep. The ref caught it mid way. In the very next exchange I got hit with an up elbow that split my forehead huge. I was wobbled from it and I got hit with a knee, and one more elbow to my temple. It hit the edge of my eye and cut me. I took a knee and after just a couple seconds popped back up. The ref looked at me and immediately waved it off.

Though I had got off the canvas quickly my cuts were so bad there was no need to even have the doctor look at them.

I couldn't believe that this guy could elbow at such a far range. I got out of the ring and the crowd looked at me crazy. I knew I had gnarly cuts.

"How bad is it," I asked Eric.

"Man, it's the worst I've seen," he said.

I got to the back. They laid me on a table and stuck me with a needle.

"This going to hurt," the doctor said.

Then he hit me with some numbing agent.

I got stitched up and bandages got put over it.

"Good job," people kept saying to me after. "America!"

I couldn't feel any of my cuts and didn't feel my hernia either, I had a lot of adrenaline going. I grabbed another bag of soda and sat back in the crowd to catch the final of the tournament, my opponent Yacine versus Aikpracha.

Aikpracha stopped him too. He was on a terror. I knew I was not even close to his level and thankful I didn't draw him for this tournament. I was always up for fighting the best but with my hernia, going into the fight with him would not have been ideal.

I went to say bye and thank you to Mr. Pong and he told me to meet him back at Lumpinee in two days to get paid. He told me that I was going to get a TV bonus for a KO, and for the amount of stitches I got. I was surprised.

I was able to get a ride back in a luxury van with a media

group called Elite Boxing. They were shooting a documentary on my friend Zidov, who was friends with the founder.

With my head split open it was best to ride back in the van and not in the back of a pick up.

I'd told the front desk girls at Fairtex prior to me leaving to please record my fight on TV and to my disappointment they did not. If you google Toyota Muay Thai tournaments, almost all of the fights over the last eight years are up...except our tournament. The only video I could find of the tournament was from the audience of my first fight. It was a girlfriend of the guy I was fighting and just before I got the KO, she turned away along with the camera and it cut out. One of my most memorable fights was gone.

When I got back to camp all the trainers and their families greeted me with a warm welcome.

"Boss you fight Toyota," the kids said to me over and over.

"Yes, Yes I did," I replied.

Apidej came by and gave me a hug. *"Geng mak* manager".

CHALLENGER

L eaving Fairtex was hard, even though my last couple months weren't the best. The business seemed to be on its way to a close and nothing I could do was going to bring it back.

As a manager, I had gone through a Thailand political crisis during my time, all the big fighters were taken to Pattaya, and many gyms were starting to be built and modernized in central Bangkok.

I always enjoyed training with camp visitors from all around the World and met many great friends. I enjoyed being a part of someone's journey whether it be escaping something back home, losing weight, or getting the chance to fight in Thailand. I was going to miss getting snacks and pizza for the factory workers kids and the trainers kids. I was going to miss having a beer with the locals across the street from camp.

I know some people could look at this and say, "What about the loyalty to the camp?"

I had put a lot of effort into my work at the camp but it wasn't enough. I don't think I ever got the trainers' respect as a fighter. Maybe they just saw me as a hobbyist because I worked at the desk all the time.

There wasn't the same enthusiasm as a couple years ago. They'd taken superstars Nareupol, Yodsaenklai and Kaew Fairtex to Pattaya.

I also didn't want to be there when the doors eventually closed. Make no mistake, it was hard.

Before I left I gave Apidej's son Neung a Texas belt buckle that my grandpa had given me as a token of appreciation for him training me. He loved western wear and it wasn't really available in Thailand. Even though we had some differences the trainers all came around and were nice on my last few days and told me to come back and visit.

After spending a little over a year and a half in Thailand working and competing I returned home to Houston, Texas late April 2011. I was happy to get back to Texas and enjoyed some time off relaxing and eating some American food. After about two weeks being in the states, I got a call from one of my old friends to work in his camp for his upcoming UFC fight. He was based in a little suburb area just outside of Oklahoma City. I was just bouncing around locally in Houston, teaching wherever just to make some extra money. A week after being in Oklahoma I got an email about being on a Muay Thai reality show called The Challenger. The Challenger was supposed to be the follow up to the widely popular Muay Thai reality show The Contender.

I had made an alright name for myself as an American competing in Thailand in The Challenger Qualifier 8-Man in Pattaya and in events like the Toyota Cup. I was really excited to get out and test myself against some top international fighters. I had to do some Skype interviews with some of the show producers. The talent scout told me I needed to have more character and be more of a person I'm not, arrogant, and cocky. In the middle of the interview the main producer had to take a quick break from the Skype call.

"Mike! You gotta be more confident; tell him you'll knock out all these guys," the talent scout said. "None of them have your boxing pedigree"

I started laughing but said fuck it and went into an act. I wasn't really confident I would get on the show after the Skype interviews though.

I think I was kind of a wild card getting on the show, because I was on a flight three days after I got the contract sent to me. Because of the non-disclosure, I couldn't tell anyone what was going on and went straight to Kuala Lumpur, Malaysia.

It was a weird arrival. They put us up in a hostel like apartment in the city with no restaurants, or grocery nearby. It was three complex towers stacked on top of each other with shops at the bottom.

There was no timeline of what was coming up or anything. I knew one thing I was heavy from being home for a bit and enjoying Tex Mex and BBQ. I needed to get outside and start running. I ran around these apartments and started seeing some others running too over the next couple of days. I didn't really make eye contact with anyone just kind of stayed in my own lane. At night some of the show's staff would grab a couple of us and take us down to a restaurant for food. We would eat Malaysian food, mainly black stews from a Tong Sui vendor and some other peanuts with rice dishes with fried chicken that I needed to avoid. I had no clue what it was. A few of us would speak at dinner and all had the same question.

"What the fuck is going on, and how long are we going to be in these apartments?"

They were very similar to college dorms. The whole floor of rooms shared one bathroom.

After a few days of people getting upset they finally told us they would take us to the house. One of the funniest things of all this reality TV stuff was the first time they had us all walk in the house where we were staying. All of us had our stuff and they said go in. "Ok...what do we do," someone asked.

"Guys this is where you're going to be staying, go in and go to your room we have your bags on the bed! Everybody go back outside and do it again."

I laughed and realized that this could be happening a lot.

When all the fighters arrived at the house I noticed some world champion competitors for the show - Jordan Watson, Marco Pique, Madsua, Frank Giorgi, Colossa etc. Then I noticed two competitors that I had fought before in Thailand, Jason Woodham and Faizal Ramli. I also saw my fellow American Cyrus Washington. Washington, Rhyse Saliba, Jesse Miles and I all roomed together. We all got along and were pretty chilled in a relaxed room. We all were quiet and mostly read during down time. The other rooms had the characters.

The first day of training was cool, because a lot of us wanted to get in there and start dropping some kg's and shake the jet lag. I was running a lot trying to get my weight down. I probably arrived at the show at 78-80kg (172-176lbs) and fights were to take place at 72.5kg (160lbs). I knew I needed to keep running a ton, because I had the feeling I was going to be picked to fight first, being that I was an American and not a well-known name in Muay Thai.

The energy in the gym was awesome. The pads were cracking and there was not one weak dude in there hitting pads. There were great trainers as well to add to the energy. Training times and length would be altered due to photo shoots, interviews and filming. That didn't sit well with some of the fighters. Personally, I was a little bothered, so I started carrying a jump rope with me places so that I could stay on my weight loss and keep a sweat.

After two days of training and filming I believe they introduced the weapon of the week. It was a highlight on a certain aspect of fighting. For the first episode it was conditioning. We had seen in the training and running who came in top shape and who was on vacation...me. I had already been approached by some staff.

"Hey America you ready," the staff member asked.

"Yeah man for sure," I said.

"We're a little behind on production. If you had to, could you fight in a couple days," he said eyeing me.

"Yes of course!"

I started getting a sense that I was going to be first either way. We had an outdoor challenge for conditioning and it was to run as many laps as you could around this outdoor ring and on the other side a soccer goal.

No one knew how long they would have us running. Was it a better strategy to stay back and relax or be at the front and possibly burn out? No clue.

My legs were a little weak from running a lot already so I stayed in the back pack. All of a sudden they said five minutes and people started breaking out. Vuysile Colossa was ahead of everyone by a longshot and at time was the winner.

He wasn't as tall as everyone, but he was cut like diamond. There wasn't an inch of softness on his body.

For the winner of the conditioned athlete challenge he then had his choice for an opponent and it was me. I knew that I would be picked in the beginning, but first sucked. I had a feeling it was coming, but I was excited to fight anyone on this show. There were so many top guys.

The money, $100,000, on the line really inspires fighters to bring it in the matches.

The fight was the next day and I needed to make weight. Out came the sauna suit and I started alternating light jogs and elliptical to try and save my legs. Both me and my opponent were next to each other on the elliptical. The staff kept their eyes on us while we shook out the weight.

"Why are they wearing space suits next to each other, is this some sort of test," one of the staff said with a Malaysian accent.

I made weight but my legs were a little shot from all the running I did.

There wasn't much time for rest and relaxation on the day of the big fight. It was hectic. We were booked to do a press conference for the announcement of the show, the day of the fight. I wasn't too happy but was out of my control.

After that was done we went back to the villa. Colossa and I had to head up to where the fight was being filmed, but I still wanted food, so they took me to the mall. To my disappointment there was no spaghetti so I went to a Kenny Rogers Chicken and got a chicken plate. I peeled off all the fried skin and ate, definitely not something I would choose fight day.

Upon arriving at the venue I got with the trainers and went through the standard pre fight, hands wrapped, Thai oil, and Challenger outfit on. I was warmed up and ready but there was a long wait before we ended up coming out for our fight. Being the first fight of the series I'm sure there were a lot of kinks and such that needed to be worked out before we came out for the fight. From the time I was told get ready you're coming out, to the actual time I walked out to the ring was close to two hours. I'm not complaining, it is the fight game. The unexpected is usual.

Colossa came into the competition in great shape and really brought it. Round one went to Colossa, but I did have my moments. Round two I started off well and landed some nice techniques and caught a kick and got a highlight reel sweep on him. Right after that he took control of the round and ended up scoring a flash knockdown. I wasn't rocked, I just didn't see it. Round three I could feel I was down in the fight so I started getting real aggressive and was looking for a cut to try and turn the fight around.

I started throwing more elbows and a couple landed, but no damage. Colossa sensed I didn't have anything for him that night and started turning it up more. He started doing damage on my legs. He was landing well and eventually dropped me in my corner from leg kicks. The ref stopped the match even though I got up, and I don't blame him. I could have continued, but Colossa had my number that night, and my legs just weren't there.

I couldn't think of anything worse than going to a reality show and being eliminated in the first episode. I had to film a shot of me going into a hallway of all the athlete's photos and hang my *mongkol* above my photo hanger. I was to tell my story, look at my photo as the first one eliminated, hang my *mongkol* on hanger #1 and out the double doors.

"I've let down the American Muay Thai community back home," I said. "But I'll be back."

They put me in a nice hotel for the night and didn't let me say bye to the other fighters at the fight house.

I was on board a flight the next morning back home.

Being home after the loss was one of my first of three rough patches mentally in fighting. I had a non-disclosure agreement with the show and couldn't really talk about the show.

"Hey man didn't you just leave out to go film a reality show?"

"Yeah I'm back early," I said. Then there was the next question.

"Well what happened...," they would ask. Then a long pause. "Well I guess your back tells me something."

I was embarrassed and the show hadn't even aired yet. I could already hear Americans talking.

"Why did they pick this guy? He's not the best for USA, he sucks."

I went out and did some drinking a few days after I got back. Then I got a call from one of my long time BJJ friends that told me there was a new gym opening near San Marcos, a college party town. I was asked if I was available for a seminar for the opening.

One of my best friend's wife reminded me about one of her friends who was out that way. I gave her a ring and told her I would be in Austin for the weekend and asked if we could get dinner and drinks. She was a nice girl from my hometown. She said yes and we were to meet at a Mexican restaurant that night. Seminar went great and we were back at my friend's apartment complex at around 1pm and we were hanging poolside and of course everyone was drinking and partying. We got through a bottle of rum by 2pm and were at the liquor store to get another. I don't drink rum and had no idea why we were drinking so much that early in the afternoon. Secondly, I was supposed to meet this girl in Austin later.

I arrived at the Mexican restaurant and of course I had to get a couple margaritas. I had some serious anxiety issues going that day and alcohol usually does the trick calming me. Problem is this place only had one size glass and it was really small. I had one, then I had too many. I almost forgot that one of my favorite underground alt country acts was in town and I had mentioned to her about going. She said that she had told some friends too and we were going to head over. It was at this time that the alcohol kicked in, and when I say kicked in, I mean that I was a mess.

I got a stare from the doorman and knew that I was not in good condition. We got in there and I shouldn't have anymore but of course, I had a beer. I got pulled on the dance floor and the girl says lets two-step. Now if you're not from Texas it's pretty much the easiest dance you can do and everyone in Texas is required to know it. I was so drunk that I couldn't even two step. My friend, the lead singer, looked out to the crowd and had a chuckle mid song at my condition. It wasn't too much longer and we were out of there. I was wishing that the night would be over but they all wanted to continue on to another bar.

I was completely canned and we were all at a table and everyone kept asking me about Thailand.

"How were the ladyboys," one friend said.

"How was the food," another asked.

"What happened with the fight?"

They then ask about what all the dancing was before a fight and the praying and I explained in my drunkenness what it was all about. I then asked them all to bow their heads and *wai* while I flicked water above them all and did a pre-fight prayer.

I woke up feeling absolutely garbage.

I had brief moments of remembrance going to the girl's house and just going to sleep on the couch. I immediately grabbed everything, apologized and left. I was embarrassed and was done with this being sad drinking bullshit. Though it was summer I layered up and sweated the whole way back to Houston.

Back in home I went back to training. I was mad with myself. I started really focusing on my conditioning as that is something fighters always have control of. You may not have the best pad men or sparring partners but you can get your ass out and run.

I got my walk around weight down considerably and was in really good shape. Most of us from the Challenger show regularly kept up with each other on Facebook. A couple had told me that they were invited back for the Challenger finale. I didn't think there was any way I was getting asked back after getting booted first episode but I was hungry and sent an email to the WMC. I expressed interest and was eager to go back and show the viewers of the show that I am better than what was seen on one episode.

The producer called me.

"We want to bring back Vuyisile Colossa…"

"Two of the guys were approached for the bout and for reasons undisclosed weren't able to do it," he said. "You want the rematch?"

There was even a storyline to it. American fighter was so embarrassed from being eliminated from the first episode he has come back seeking revenge. He said a lot of the boys they were going to use for the final were in Thailand and that it would be a financial strain to fly in people outside for the finale.

"Not a problem," I said, "I'll fly myself out."

It was probably that statement that got me back. I was that determined. I flew myself out to Kuala Lumpur, Malaysia on my own dollar to show I was better than what was aired. They told me that they would try to get me $1,000 for travel which in the end would be just a wash.

"No problem," I said. "How many fighters out there would fight a World Champion for nothing?

Because all of us fought in weights above and below the Challenger the people brought back fought in different categories. Marco Pique versus Mustapha Abdallah was for 75kg WMC MAD Title, Jason Woodham versus Faizal Ramli was for 70 kg WMC MAD, the shows $100,000 main event was for 72.5 WMC World Championship, and I believe Colossa and I was for 72.5 WMC MAD Title. I don't give a shit about all the belts I just wanted to face top guys.

When we arrived at the weigh-ins the fighters, staff, etc; were all surprised.

"Hey Captain America you came in shape this time," everyone said.

I was. And I was determined.

The event was in the Negara Stadium which is a pretty big domed arena in Kuala Lumpur. The card had some local Malaysian rivalries and four bouts from the Challenger. The stadium seemed like The Stadium for the city. It had to be the biggest venue. It looked like the Astrodome but a little smaller. There was quite a big crowd there and they sectioned it off so it looked bigger on TV.

My fight was up. I don't remember much about walking out or entering the ring. You can say that I was kind of in the zone. It wasn't until the bell rang that I started somewhat putting the fight together. I realized I was in the smallest ring I'd ever fought in. I came out firing first and used good boxing and solid left kicks. The crowd roared when one of my left kicks landed very heavily.

The round was over and I think I had it won. Second round was all Colossa. I just remember not using my distance anymore, not using the jab or body kicks. The third round started and I believe I got caught in an exchange and dropped. I was still good and in the fight, but my head wasn't really all there. I believe It was a combination of both repeated head shots and low kicks that made me take a knee. I was getting up.

"Come on America. Get up. Finish this. Come on," I heard someone yell.

I got up one more time and fought back but was just battered more and the ref waved it off. Colossa really mixed up his boxing and low kicks well on me. He had my number.

"Michael, now that was a better fight," Colossa told me after.

Again I got bested though this time it didn't feel as bad. I mean don't get me wrong I am very hard on myself for losing but this seemed to get more of the people's respect. Coaches, fighters came up to me and gave me some praise.

I came back out and watched Jordan Watson and Tum Madsua for the finale and $100,000.

It was a great match with Madsua cutting Jordan over the forehead. It was a close one but Madsua pulled it off. All the castmates took some photos in the arena and then we headed back to the hotel to change up. Some people from the show had told us that a big area of nice club was rented out and that there was going to be a nice spread for food.

When I got to the hotel I realized my face was swollen and discolored. My leg was chopped up. I came out to prove that I was a better fighter than what was aired on TV, and I accomplished that but I still came up short. I still lost. I still was not World Champion level. It's something that I think a lot of people don't realize in this game. Not everyone is going to be elite world level.

There was a big line to get in and we had special wrist-bands to take us to our designated area. As I walked up, I noticed it was a lot of the show staff but none of the fighters. I was pretty hungry and noticed that our dinner was just a charcuterie spread of meats and cheese already passed over by random people? I was in one of those hangry moods and that wasn't going to do it. I said thank you to some of the people and walked back to my hotel.

Right as I left the club I saw some of the fighters entering.

"Where you going, America," they asked me.

"Man it's not my thing up there and no food," I replied.

They dragged me back in and I showed them our area and three of the four of us were right back out. A few of us decided to go over to Jordan Watson's room. He'd ordered a bunch of room service and we all threw down on some more booze. If I remember right we got a lot of pizza. We all hung out and shot the shit for a while talking about what was next for everybody.

I finally headed off and then saw some more friends by the pool. It must have been 4-5am at this time. Everybody was pretty drunk, but still going. Marco Pique was telling me that he was finally going to go home to Suriname next month and that he was going to have a homecoming show on Christmas. He said that Nieky Holzken and Jemyma Betrian were going to be on the card too. They wanted to have an international flair and asked if anyone had approached me about it?

"Eric Haycraft was looking at me and Cyrus Washington as opponents," I told him. "But I don't know who for who."

We all ended up drinking till sunrise, knowing that we are probably fighting each other in a month. That's Muay

Thai though, it's rare anyone is ever mad or disrespectful before or after a fight.

I was an American on the show who got kicked off first, brought back for the finale and lost again. I took two losses. It was tough for me to get over that but it better prepared me for my future in the sport. It opened a lot of doors for me internationally as well.

I wouldn't take it back.

11

PHOTOS

Featured In The Fairtex Equipment Catalog

Doing The Wai Kru At Lumpinee Stadium

Walking Out To the Ring With Bagpipes

At Fairtex Bangplee

Jumping Knee In Canada

With Yoknoi Fairtex former Lumpinee Champion

Toyota Cup Poster

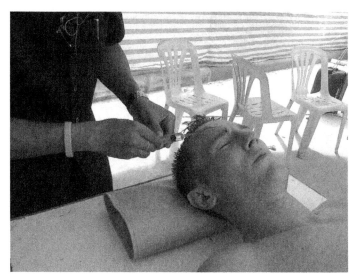

Getting Sewn Up At The Toyota Cup

With My Cornerman Eric Gerber

Fairtex Bangplee Staff And I

Thailand VS USA

Finals of the I-1 Tournament in Hong Kong

Giving out gear at the Cambodian gym

12

SURINAME TO GLORY

I t was myself, Eric Haycraft, Cyrus Washington, and a guy named Ron Ritter I believe, meeting in Miami to fly to Aruba and then straight to Suriname. Suriname used to be a Dutch colony. So it is a country that still speaks primarily Dutch. There is a very heavy influence of Dutch kickboxing there and many superstars have come from Suriname: Tyrone Sponge, Rayen Simson, Marco Pique, Andy Ristie, Melvin Manhoef and more. Eric Haycraft, the "Dutch Connection," had put word out to me before my rematch with Colossa on the Challenger Finale. He was looking to take some Americans down to Suriname for some fights. It was going to be a big show with Nieky Holzken and Marco Pique headlining. I was game. I really liked both of their styles and really wanted to test myself against it.

Dutch style is more hands to kicks. Rarely do they block with their legs and they always return with their hands. In kickboxing that's okay because if you block a body kick with your arms it is not considered a score. Both Holzken and Pique had crisp boxing that tied into their kickboxing.

When we were closing out at The Challenger Finale, Marco and I hung out and talked about fighting. He was excited to go back to his home for a fight. My fight with Marco Pique was the first Muay Thai fight in the country's history and the only Muay Thai fight on the card.

This fight was on Christmas eve. I had to tell my family, "sorry I'm going to go fight in South America for Christmas."

They had all the fighters at the hotel overlooking the huge and I mean the biggest and fastest, flowing, river I have seen in person, the Suriname river. There was a big pool area where it seemed like everyone was on vacation, all the coaches and fighters' entourage were out having some drinks and the music was loud. Everyone had matching gear on and it was a who's who of Dutch kickboxing.

The weather was really nice and Eric and I went sight-seeing around the city of Paramaribo the capital. We went into historic downtown where there was cool Dutch histor-ical architecture from back in the colonial period there. There were old wooden boats everywhere and fishermen. We continued on heading to a historic cathedral that I wanted to see and all of a sudden just walking around in the street was the kickboxing legend Rayen Simson. Rayen held wins over many legends in the sport Ramon Dekker, and Lamsongkram Chuwattana and at one point was ranked #2 in Lumpinee Stadium. He knew we were there for the fights.

Eric and I stuck out really easy. We were the only two white dudes in the city. Seeing him led Eric and I to talk.

He'd spent time in Holland. He was the most knowledgeable coach about real kickboxing in the USA. His blonde flat top hair made him easy to spot, that and the bright orange tracksuit displaying the logo of his Kentucky gym.

"How do we get better at the game," Haycraft asked me with his southern drawl.

"We keep on playing," I said. "And get experience."

It was one of the topics we'd discussed for years over and over. We've always been trying to grow the sport and get better in the US.

American Muay Thai fighters need more experience to compete internationally.

A day before the weigh-ins they brought us to the city's news station to film a press conference. We all put on some blue polos with a local car dealership logo on it and the home team all wore red polos. We were told to talk a little bit but in Muay Thai and kickboxing it is very respectful most of the time. The heavyweight from Suriname was the only one that was letting our American have it. He was saying he was going to knock him out in the first.

Marco and I just did some normal back and forth but all respectful. It was pretty uneventful from the fighters' standpoint. The one thing that got going was they had local rap artists and DJ's doing like a celebrity fight. Those were pretty funny because they all talked trash really good but couldn't fight at all.

The weigh-ins were held in front of a shopping mall in downtown Paramaribo. They had a DJ and a hype man getting the crowd going. My opponent came up to me, whose coach was also helping promote the card and told all of us the Suriname people love drama so after we check weight to do an intense stare down and get the crowd behind it. So I hit the scale and then Marco and I have this stare down right there in the street and the crowd was excited. The promoter, a tall black man with dreadlocks, told us that the crowd was really excited for the fights.

The crowd was more excited for the celebrity fights but that's ok I guess. A good crowd is a crowd and I don't care which I fight in.

We got to the venue and it was packed! There must have been two to three thousand people in there and they were a loud crowd. There were three of us Americans. Cyrus and I have been around the world together in the fight game and we were both cool.

Cyrus and I just chilled in the back. He's well built and athletic guy with a dynamic Tae Kwon Do style that he's fused into his Muay Thai. Cyrus had broad shoulders and hardly spoke a word. He wasn't the type of guy to initiate conversation. I had a lot of respect for the name he made for himself at the time in Thailand.

We had known each other before The Challenger and I even went to China to help corner him in the past.

The DJ came in and asked if we had any music we wanted to come out to? I was feeling some DMX that day and wanted to do the intro to 'It's Dark And Hell Is Hot' album. It's a hype song. The DJ said he had it and we were good. Eric Haycraft had me over to start wrapping.

"Some of these first fights might go quick," he said as he wrapped my hands. He was good at it, experienced.

Since there were celebrities, he wrapped us all early. He cornered us all.

I was about to walk through the curtains and before the music hit they told us to start walking.

"Hold on the music hasn't come on," I said.

"Step on up," they said.

I started going at the very beginning of the song when DMX was just talking.

'Dog that's my mans in them, Rough Ryders'

DMX's intro went over and over for about 40 seconds. The actual song didn't start. I was just a ghostly white guy coming out with DMX just talking shit as his walkout.

Where was the damn song? So bad.

I got to the ring and Eric held down the ropes as I did my prayer and jumped over. I push down and think he's still pushing down and I throw myself over the ropes but he was no longer holding down the rope! I went completely horizontal and fell completely flat, a belly flop on the ring. The crowd lost their shit laughing.

Marco's music hit and the crowd was back to hype.

"Well that's over with," Eric said. He came over to me and put in my mouth piece and gave me some water.

The fight started with some feeling out and then we started exchanging. Though it was Muay Thai rules it was just a three round fight. That took away the feeling out. The first round was close and it was pretty even.

The second round started and we went after it again. It stayed pretty even until I ate an overhand right hand that hit off the top of my head. It made this weird buzzing feeling through my body. I got right back up and wasn't wobbly, it was the weirdest thing. The second round closed. It was definitely 10-8 for my opponent.

The third round began and knowing I was down I started throwing some elbows and they started landing too. On two or three exchanges I was finishing with elbows and on the very last exchange I back straight out and eat a left kick right on the outside of my right forearm and it went completely numb. I looked back at the video and I smiled and literally shake my arms as if I'm shaking it off and then fire a retreating shitty right kick. Something was really wrong with my right arm. I kept fighting on. I took a knee on another overhand right. Took a second and was like damn, I lost. I got up and didn't know if the fight had been stopped or the bell rang but the fight came to a close. I actually never asked and then years later I saw L TKO RD 3 and also see L Decision.

Regardless, I lost.

I had really good moments but didn't stick to it. I was still a young man in the game when it came to experience. At the time of this fight Marco quadrupled me in experience and had fought the likes of Jongsanan, Buakaw, etc. He knew how to keep calm and it was something I learned from the fight. I would get too antsy when something would go right and sometimes that leaves you open. That's what happened to me.

In the back Eric asked me to see the doctor about my right arm. Me being the stupid too tough for my own good I said," I'm good."

My arm was numb and my adrenaline was going. My self test was literally a couple pushups to see if my arm was ok. I was able to do them with no pain. I threw on some sweats and put on a jacket to assist Eric with Cyrus' fight with Nieky. Nieky at the time was at the top of his game. Cyrus had just had some big wins in China, and Belarus but under Muay Thai rules. This bout was to be under kickboxing where Nieky had much more experience.

Nieky used his pressure and shell to stalk Cyrus and walk him down.

This was my first time to see a true kickboxer versus Muay Thai / Taekwondo stylist. Cyrus ate a big liver shot and made the count at the end of the bell. The second started and Nieky continued the pressure. I could tell Cyrus was uncomfortable with kickboxing but Cyrus is always dangerous. All of a sudden Nieky hits a knee on his head that split him badly. He took a knee and the blood poured. Eric threw in the towel not to stop the fight but for the ref to press to Cyrus' head. Cyrus is as tough as they come. He wanted to keep fighting.

Cyrus' head exploded with blood. They called it then and there.

The fight was over. Eric went with Cyrus to the hospital which I heard was a nightmare just to get stitches. It took them six hours.

I on the other hand was taken by limo with all the other fighters to the after party. I talked a little bit to Jemyma Betrian who was the only female fight on the card about fighting in the USA. She would occasionally fight on Dennis Warner's shows in California or Vegas cards. I talked with Marco and a few others but they were back home and like celebrities. I had a couple drinks and went home early. I wasn't in the mood.

We didn't have a flight back till late the next day so we spent the day at the pool just talking shop with all the Dutch teams. A lot of the Dutch teams took the trip as a vacation and stuck around. I learned a lot that day at the pool on training and fight philosophies from Nieky Holzken and his trainer. They were very kind but no bullshit. They gave me their card and told me to contact them if I was serious about kickboxing. I learned a lot. Experts gave me a breakdown on my fight. They told me my strengths and weaknesses. It made me feel better about going forward.

"You're pretty good America," they told me. "You're just not at the level yet."

Of course with a lot of my travels there was a lot of

asking me about Texas. I would always laugh. There were a couple of big Dutch guys that were so keen on going to Texas.

"I want to shoot guns like a cowboy," they said. "I want to eat BBQ and ride on a horse." I had a few drinks with them all and enjoyed the day.

We flew back to Miami all together. Everyone had split up and Eric came up to me.

"There's gonna be a new big kickboxing organization coming out," he told me.

It was going to be bigger than K1. They were going to have an inaugural tournament but wanted to have a couple Americans in the tournament to guarantee advancement. He told me I needed to focus more on kickboxing and that I may be an alternate for the tournament. We talked and I told him that it was eye opening to see high level kickboxing in person.

It's a totally different sport than Muay Thai. Don't get me wrong I love Muay Thai but kickboxing is different. I needed to change my game to be successful in that sport. I wasn't training properly. Also I didn't have experience in the game. I didn't know how to deal with everything.

I was home and back to teaching but my arm was still killing me. I went to some sports medicine place and the guy did a cold laser on it and temporarily it felt better but not much. I thought some rest would do the trick.

It was about three weeks after the fight and I thought I could move around with some of the guys at the school I was teaching at. I was moving around throwing some kicks and I threw a light one-two. The right landed straight on the guy's forehead and my right arm just shot up in extreme pain. I yelled something I don't remember and I just jumped out of the ring and just started power walking around the whole gym. I finally stopped and looked to see that my arm was bent. I definitely broke something. I drove myself one armed to the emergency room because again I was too tough and stupid to have someone take me.

I got there and they took me in for an X-ray. I broke my ulna, forearm.

"From the looks of the X-ray it was already broken and had begun to heal," the doctor said. "But then you broke it even more."

The fight with Pique there was a slight fracture. I didn't get it looked at and then nearly had the bone come out of my arm from light sparring weeks later.

They had me in a cast from my hand all the way up to the top of my bicep and lower shoulder bent like an L. It was disastrous. Taking showers, driving, teaching Muay Thai was awful. The one good thing about it was that I started learning to properly block left kicks! I would even tell my class as a "joke,"

"Hey if you want to block them the wrong way you'll end up like me."

I was angry telling the same old story as to why I was in a cast. I was angry that I couldn't work out. I was angry I couldn't hold pads for private lessons. I was embarrassed wearing that big cast. It was only about three to four weeks and I was to be in the cast for eight!

I got a call from Eric that one of the Americans may not be taking the Glory opportunity and that I needed to prepare like I might be getting in. There wasn't a date set.

My good friend Andrew Craig had just signed to the UFC and I was excited to start working with him as a striking coach. So much shit was about to happen and my mind was racing.

I was getting too stir crazy. One night I had finally had it. I drove from my apartment over to my parents' house and went into their garage. I got a hacksaw and went to work on getting that cast off. I know what you're thinking. I am just a crazy person. What am I going to do? Arm not healed and can't punch nor hold pads. It took me a couple hours to get that thing off and when I finally did it felt so good. I made a fist and felt a little burn but not much. My spirits were immediately lifted.

I reached out to a friend who got me a good deal on an Ultrasound Bone Growth Stimulator through my insurance that I had with a gym I was teaching at. It was a little device where you would put the jelly on the spot of the injury and then put a cold magnet like thing on it that was connected by a coiled line to a machine. It would run on 20 minute sessions. I would do this three times per day and I took a ton of Calcium and different mineral supplements to speed healing. I kept it wrapped in an ace bandage. After about two or three weeks there was no more pain and I could feel the buildup in the healing.

Or so I thought.

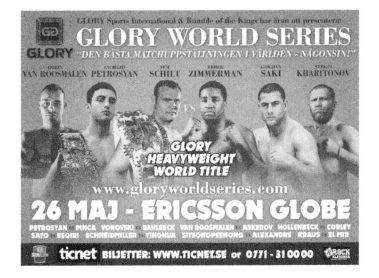

After K1, Glory took the spot as the number one kickboxing event in the world. The inaugural event was a 16 man 70kg tournament.

It was held in Stockholm Sweden.

The top two Americans at the time were Ky Hollenbeck

and Chaz Mulkey. Both were slated to be in the tournament. Glory wanted to put the two Americans in the first round of the tournament so that it guaranteed an American was in the final eight. The two were training partners so Chaz decided to withdraw if I remember correctly. I was the number three and got the call. I was very excited for the opportunity, and knew I had a serious challenge in Ky. I had trained with him once before and he was very strong. The rest of the tournament was stacked with a who's who of kickboxing; Albert Krauss, Soto, Fabio Pinca, Petrosyan, and Robin Van Roosmalan.

Leading up to the event I needed to be at my best but I took some regrettable steps in getting ready. I tried a new diet that was sponsored by a pretty famous MMA dietician and I believe I was one of the first to test. The diet didn't have much variety to it and wasn't very enjoyable. I drank and ate stuff that wasn't beneficial for my energy levels. Diet knowledge is way better now.

I have traveled the world and ate just about everything. I am not the type to complain, I mean I ate rats in Thailand after my first pro fight. The dietician has changed since but I felt like I was training on antibiotics the whole camp, just drained.

Training was about as good as it was going to get for Houston in 2012. I would scramble up guys from all over the city to try and get some Muay Thai and kickboxing looks. MMA striking dominated in the city so it was very hit or miss. For being in the fourth largest city in the USA we had zero active professional Muay Thai or kickboxing athletes. There weren't many pad men in the city that could hold for Muay Thai or kickboxing. I reached out to Bob Perez to see if he could hold for me a couple days out of the week and watch some sparring and drilling. He had a couple of students that had similar build to Ky so I would tell them to mimic his style. Ky didn't have any video out available. I was showing them how to be him amusingly.

I believe Ky comes from a gymnastic and wrestling background and is built like it. He's super strong, square, and very unorthodox. He bounces around like a gymnast and a lot of his punches are the type you wouldn't see in a boxing match. He throws up jabs and wild hooks but he was very effective.

This camp is when it finally set in that I could not be the fighter that I was in Thailand or even close to that here in the US. I was teaching classes, and scrambling to get decent workouts in. In Thailand I could train twice a day with a solid pad man, clinch with the kids and foreign visitors, basically be in a solid routine. I regret taking a lot of the fights that I did when I returned from Thailand. I wanted to still be in the mix. I loved fighting the best opposition because it brought out the best in me both mentally and physically but if you're not having a world class fight camp, how are you to compete against world class talent?

As the date approached I asked my boxing coach if he could go with me but he had already committed to a big boxing show. I asked Eric Haycraft who had cornered me in Suriname in 2011, but he couldn't. I asked my 2009 USA IFMA coaches, Kirian Fitzgibbons and Rudi Ott, and both couldn't make it. It was not good. I ended up taking my roommate at the time, UFC Fighter, Andrew Craig. He's tall, and looked like a surfer. His shoulder length hair was a dark brown which was always corn rowed for his MMA bouts.

It would be his first time cornering for a kickboxing/Muay Thai fight.

Training wise I felt ok, not good, but ok, but the weight wasn't coming off like I wanted. Nevertheless, Andrew and I boarded our flights and headed over to Stockholm, Sweden. After a couple of outdoor workouts and runs, my weight hit a wall and I had to resort to a lot of sauna time.

Sitting in the sauna is rough. If you do too much it dries your brain out. It makes it hard to replenish. It's really a last resort for cutting weight. I like it leading up to fights though for brief periods. It helps get a sweat on. Crashing into the sauna multiple times like I did was really bad. I didn't have a choice though. I was locked up and wasn't losing any weight.

I would feel chest pressure, and have to step out of the hot box. My stints would only last ten minutes before the tightness in the chest came in. My body felt squeezed dried and my brain was like a ball in a rattling pinball machine.

Muay Thai and kickboxing culture is relaxed. We're all connected somehow in Muay Thai and kickboxing. Whether it be we fought on a show together in the past or we faced the same foe. We were in the sauna with a lot of the fighters of the tournament David Kiria, my opponent Ky, and others. This fight was the most sauna time I had ever done so I got to see a lot of people.

In the morning I went over to the scale and saw that I was 2.3 lbs over and I was pretty dried out. I figured I was going to lose a pound in my sleep and be good for my weigh-in. I woke up and saw I was still 1.5 lb over. So I layered up and figured it would float off till early afternoon. We made our way to the weigh in and just before I got on the scale I went to the bathroom. I had nothing but a few dehydrated drops come out. My manhood looked nonexistent.

They began calling all the fighters to the stage to get ready. My fight was one of the first ones called and I went up with Andrew.

"Bring the towel," I told him. "This is going to be close."

The tournament was 70kg (154lbs) with 0 weight allowance. I got on the scale in some lucky Irish boxers and the scale said 154.3!

"Damnit," I said.

Andrew held the towel in front of me. My body and manhood were so depleted.

"Fuck it," I said.

I dropped my boxers and weighed in right on the dot.

We did the usual stare down and posed for the cameras and hit the water. We had to sit through the rest of the press conference. Afterwards we stormed out to the city to grab some good food. My stomach was so shrunk I had to eat a tiny meal, rest a bit and have another small meal.

As I sat in the hotel room Ky my opponent messaged me a picture of his post weigh in feast he had gathered at the local grocery and then a picture of the scale he was up in weight considerably. This guy had cuts down.

So this is it, we are making the walk to the stadium. It was at the Erikson Globe in Sweden, well the hall next to it. I took photos outside of it because I was so excited. Giorgio Petrosyan, Fabio Pinca, Semmy Schilt all the big names taking part in a historic card. I walked into my dressing room and sat and took it in. The dressing room was shared with me and two other people. I would see famous guys in the hallway but I was in my own little world. The fight room itself was a basic event conference room that fit 1500-2000 people but it was still historic to me.

I didn't have any of my go-to coaches so I wrapped my hands myself. It's no good wrapping by yourself. You need certain help, like you need someone holding the pad on the knuckles down. I don't think you can make it 50% as good as if someone did it for you.

I told Andrew what combos to hold and started warming up and got ready for my biggest fight to date.

My walkout had the theme from "The Good The Bad, And The Ugly" and flames shot out as I went down the ramp. I chose it because I was from Texas on an international card. I was like Clint Eastwood in the Man with No Name series. I was a fighter with no following on the international circuit. I don't think anyone but myself put it together. It was complete silence. When I walked into the ring, I almost felt like I was asleep. It was so quiet. The announcers Mauro Ranallo and Stephen Quadros thought it was a cool entrance song in our pre fight interview and it totally tanked and put the crowd to bed.

The fight started and I got right out and pumped a double jab and a low kick. That was it. That's all I landed in the entire fight.

Shortly after I ate a right hand on the temple. I was wobbly but still standing. The referee came in and gave me an eight count. Knowing I was wobbly I shelled up and let him come to punch on the gloves a bit to get my fogginess out. After a few punches the referee stopped the bout. I was furious. I wasn't all there. Sure it could have been stopped. But why not let me at least get knocked down? That was the end of it.

The biggest fight of my career stopped in under a minute. I went back to the dressing room and pushed a chair down. I sat down just completely done. I really didn't have the words. I went out and watched the fights from behind a curtain. I didn't want the crowd to see me. What could they say? Good fight? Good Job? It was fucking terrible.

Our flight was the next morning, pretty early.

"No matter what happens," I told Andrew. "We need to get to the airport on time."

We had to be out the door at the hotel no later than 7am to catch the flight.

Then we set off into the night.

I struck Stockholm with full force.

Being that I didn't hydrate all the way from the weigh in, I was drunk pretty quick. We bounced around and ended up at this indoor outdoor bar that was between two streets. I ended up seeing some of the people from the card there. I saw Ky there.

"I wish I could have given a better look," I told him.

I was pissed off. The bar was full of media people. We didn't talk much about the fight. What was there to talk about?

Ky ended up going with us to another bar. People recognized us from the fights and told us to go to this old cathedral that had been converted into a rave. We walked right up and it was pretty fucking amazing inside. There was crazy lighting with an old creepy cathedral feel. I was pretty incoherent at that time. I remember this though right after we all got our first drink we all went separate into the madness. Somehow we all came together again and made it back to the hotel.

I woke up feeling awful with no idea what time it was. I ran down to Andrew's room.

"Why are we missing this flight," I screamed as I got to his door.

The door was slightly open. I opened it slowly not sure what I was walking into. I saw him on the couch lying upside down vertically in his underwear, feet to the ceiling, head on the floor with the alarm going off right next to his ear!

"What the hell man," I said, shaking him.

He had no idea what was going on. I would later do something very similar when I cornered him in Brazil.

I figured I was such an embarrassment to Glory, I didn't even want to bother telling them I missed their flight.

"Let's put our money together and book something," I told Andrew once he was coherent enough to listen. He ended up putting up at least 70% on the spot and I had to wait to get home to clear my earnings. To keep the price modest on trying to leave the next day we had to take the long way home with several stops through Germany, Finland, Chicago, Houston.

We ended up in Germany for the first layover. I was hungover, pissed and with a stein of beer and a chocolate iced donut.

"You know what losing looks like," I asked Andrew.

"No. What?"

"This is what losing in one minute at the biggest kick-boxing promotion in the world looks like."

When I got home, everything was just setting in. There was the online shit talk. The let down of people in the community. The let down of people who are close to you. Most don't understand all you go through in the fight game.

"Did you win or lose," is all everyone asks.

This time it was harder to tell people. I just fought on one of the biggest shows in the world and got TKO'd in a minute. I was done. I went into a bad place for a while. I wanted so much to still be in the mix of international competition but it wasn't realistic for me anymore. I decided at the moment that I was going to hang the gloves. I regrettably wrote out one of those long, bullshit Instagram posts. I wrote something about how since I moved back home I hadn't been the same fighter and blah, blah, blah, time for me to retire.

It was the first time I'd considered calling it a day.

14

BOXING

I couldn't even count. Three or four losses in a row since returning back to America. Not a very good theme going on. Returning home from Thailand I was not the same fighter. I felt I still had more fight, but knew this was not the time to be taking on world champions while having lackluster training. I was also busy teaching classes, privates, and started training my roommate at the time Andrew Craig who was 1-0 in the UFC when we started back working together.

I had mornings free and didn't want to be idle. I went back to boxing, back to where I got started. I reached out to the man that got me into boxing Irish Ed Hatrick. He's a tall New York Irish cop that my dad knew. He would always invite me over to watch boxing fights growing up.

"You outta come by and do some boxing," he would say when I was a kid. He would spar with me and when I first started off he took me to some gym in Houston where I was the only white kid. That's how it all had started.

"You have to visit Lou Savarese," Hatrick told me one day. "He's got a gym in downtown Houston. I'll set you up with a meeting."

Savarese was a former heavyweight boxing champ from the Bronx and he looked it too. He had that tough guy mug together with a New York accent that he self admittedly coined his own language.

I got to the meeting and told him I had 11 Amateur Boxing matches but then got into Muay Thai heavy for five years professionally.

"I'd heard you was a Texas A & M Grad," he said. "Let's use that as your stick."

I was like what were you thinking?

I was thinking the "Irish Texas Aggie" or "Fighting Irish Aggie."

I wasn't too thrilled about the names he was thinking of but was down to get back into the winning side of fighting.

All the big money people attending fights in Texas were always oil business people and a lot of the engineers for the industry came from Texas A & M. I wasn't an engineer

MUAY THAI GRIT | 113

though. In college I boxed and fought. I ended up going to school for sports management.

Lou then introduced me to his late career trainer and co-owner of the gym, Bobby Benton. Bobby had come from a family of boxing.

His father was a champion trainer and promoter. Bobby grew up in the gym and I instantly clicked with his methods right away.

I asked them both, "So what do you think, time wise, before I could get in the ring?"

They mentioned that they just had a show and that they were going to skip a month and then return the following.

"Well how does it all work," I asked.

"Don't worry kid. We'll get you the right music."

I liked the sound of that.

I went to the gym the next Monday and they had sparring set up for Monday, Wednesday, and Friday. If you don't know, pro boxing sparring is 100% full throttle. I was the new kid in the gym and got thrown to the wolves. They had me spar against former world title contender Cedric Agnew and he made me look silly. I stayed in it though, just being tough and offering him really no work and just a sweat. It wasn't a lot but I think I got some tiny bit of respect for staying in. It was a great atmosphere to train in. The gym had a lot of history and had been open forever. It had champs from the 80's and 90's all the way up.

It reminded me of Thailand but for boxing. Both are individual sports but there's always a team atmosphere in the gym. A good spot has good training and good training partners. Some days we would do sprints together and it would get competitive. Everybody pushed each other that little extra. All the young guys wanted to be like the older champs and the older champs were always honing their tools. Everybody ran together and everyone trained at the same times.

The first bout was set and at this point I had not fought in Texas since 2007/2008 when I had fought in the Houston vs New York Amateur Boxing Gala. I started feeling all this pressure that I never felt in fighting. All these people were talking to me about my fight, and asking for tickets.

I liked it when I was fighting internationally and just showed up and put on a show. I had family and friends that wanted to come out. It was different. People called and texted about the fight when I already gave them the information, asking about my opponent, asking if I was going to knock them out. Craziness.

My first professional boxing match was set for the Houston Fencing Center. It was a small little venue. My dad and all his buddies pre gamed considerably before coming to the fights. It was their way of getting in the zone. I had tons of childhood friends I hadn't seen in years there. It was cool. I had bagpipes taking me out from the dressing room to the ring. The crowd was hype.

My opponent was southpaw and very unorthodox. The round started and he came out throwing heat for about the first 30 seconds but nothing landed cleanly for him. After I withstood a couple of his wild flurries I started tagging him. After the first right hand landed I knew he was goner. I threw a straight right he ducked out of and as he came back I landed a huge uppercut and followed it with a hook. He went out. It was the worst knockout I ever delivered. The ref began a count but the ringside doctor had already jumped into the ring. I stood in the corner as the crowd went nuts. They got him on a stool after about a minute. It was good to see he had recovered ok. The doctor had jumped in already and was checking him out. I went over and patted my opponent on the shoulder.

After the fight one of the event's sponsors had an after party and all my friends, new and old, drank the night away.

Lou, the promoter, and all the guys from the gym were there, it was a good night...or two I think.

They wanted to keep me busy so I was right back to training after the fight. My first was November 10th and they told me I would be fighting again January 10th. So I went a little light on the holidays. In boxing I fought a lot heavier than I did in Muay Thai. I figured that after all the years of fighting and cutting weight, I thought it would be healthier not to cut so much for boxing. I'm not the most elusive guy and thought with just two weapons in boxing I was going to be taking some more head punches than Muay Thai.

We were at weigh-ins for my second pro boxing fight and at the time my walk around was around 175 lbs and I was fighting super middleweight 168 lbs. I jumped on the scale and waited for them to call up my opponent. Early level pro boxing is similar to early level Muay Thai. I didn't know who I was fighting till I got to the weigh in or the fight itself.

My guy was huge.

He had a very strong physique for the weight. After having some post weigh-in food, a bit of mediocre spaghetti, I jumped on a computer to look up my opponent. I saw he had been matched against some very tough opposition and saw that he had fought as heavy as cruiserweight. No wonder he looked so big, I thought to myself.

It was fight day and I was getting the best hand wraps ever done by Bobby Benton. When I get a nice wrap put on my hands that's when I get into the zone. I started shadow boxing in them and continually made a fist. I was ready to go.

The bagpiper came into the back and asked me if I had any requests.

"I don't know, let's get a march song." I say.

We hit the walk to the ring and the bagpipes were roaring

and the crowd was going nuts. This fight was being filmed for television. I was starting to like this hometown fighting thing.

The fight started and that's when I found out I am fighting a southpaw. We opened with some bombs being thrown on both ends and I received a hellacious hook that landed flush and it did nothing.

The whole fighting heavier thing really made me more durable.

The first round ended and even though I ate a huge hook I picked him apart and had the round. During the round our heads collided and some old scar tissue pinched under my chin so I started bleeding pretty bad from there. The second round he came hard again and landed a few things but I started finding my groove and began working my uppercuts inside and lots of body work. I ended up dropping him with a body shot and he got up, and came at me like a mad man. We collided heads again and this time an old cut on my eyebrow opened up. The round closed and it looked more close of a fight I guess to the crowd because I was bleeding over my eye and my chin.

The crowd was going nuts going into the third round and again my opponent came at me hard for the first thirty seconds and then started showboating and taunting me by sticking his tongue out. I wasn't phased by this and in my head I remember thinking I was going to fuck this dude up. He backed up into a corner and started waving me to come on and dropped his lead arm and tried some philly roll taunt.

My opponent did a shoulder guard and then rolled into a horizontal shell. I nodded to acknowledge him and fucking bombed him with an overhand right. I hate taunting in fights. In my head I was screaming "Fuck you! Fuck you!"

But he got up! He folded his arm taunting again like what I hit him with was some fluke. I was a little surprised how he got up. The round ended and again the crowd was in a frenzy. I really felt like I had all of Houston and Spring with me.

In between rounds Bobby and Hollywood told me to get him out of there. I was in full agreement. They packed some Vaseline into my cuts and I got up from the stool ready to end it. I started the round hard this time and he never gained momentum again. I dropped him with body shots that really hurt him, he barely rose and at that point I came in and just smoked him with a right. As he was falling I tried to throw a hook and the ref pulled my right arm so that I couldn't reach with the hook and waved off the fight.

Bobby came in the ring and lifted me up to the crowd.

I stuck my tongue out like my opponent had been doing all fight. The place was on fire and the bagpipes were playing.

I went to the back and to do the usual taking off the wraps and wiping down myself before I laid across the table and waited for the doctor. I got four stitches on my eyebrow and eight on my chin. All while I'm getting stitches my opponent's coach is hanging around me talking about how great a fight that was and that we have to do a rematch.

"Dude I'm getting stitches. Get outta here" I said.

This event was at a nicer venue which of course brings the ticket price up and more of the who's who of Houston would come out to the fights. It was the kind of event where old businessmen sat at tables with a bunch of dolled up younger women.

Lou was really happy with the show and a lot of his high end sponsors and clients came out to the after party. I stuck around for a bit but didn't really care for the crowd.

I hid with some friends and we drank like we used to when we were younger. It was crazy to me that for my friends this was some big night out for them. They had all got married and were on their first or second kid while I was out doing this ol' fight stuff. It was good having them there for support but it also reassured me that I was not about that life yet or ever. This fight stuff was going to be in my plans for some time.

The following week the Houston Chronicle came to the gym and interviewed me for an article. They wanted to talk about how I was from Spring and went to Thailand to be a pro Muay Thai fighter and now I was back home doing pro boxing. They wanted something about being in Thailand, and the experiences I had. I never wanted to say I'm a boxer. I always like to say I'm a Muay Thai fighter now doing boxing. I knew that sounded weird.

A week later I was on ESPN radio in Houston.

"Michael Chase Corley, former Moo Thai fighter," they said introducing me.

I was like, what the fuck, why does everyone in Texas always say either Mai Thai or Moo Thai?

There seemed to be a little buzz about me in the area for my boxing. I had to wait a hot minute though. They had the next fight ready to go in April because in Houston everyone is a football fan and February is the Super bowl and then Valentine's day. Then comes March and that's rodeo in Houston, and you don't do events during rodeo in Houston. There's the biggest names in music there for two weeks, carnivals, BBQ, and party tents. You don't do events during rodeo.

I went back to training and in my first sparring session I got a really bad stinger in my neck. It took me out of sparring for two or three weeks. It must have been me turning at the wrong moment or something because I didn't really get tagged too bad that day. The first day back after that two or three weeks off I sparred this really tough Mexican style fighter who just went toe to toe with me for three straight rounds. In the third I got a hit with a shot to my ribs. As I was punching, a rib popped out. I was hurt tremendously and in the fourth round I just ran around. I could barely crouch in between the second and third rope to get out of the ring. I had an anxiety attack of sorts.

I couldn't breathe normally and just walked around the whole upstairs until I could get my breathing calmed down. I didn't want anyone to know I was hurt, but man as I was breathing, cartilage or something from around the rib was popping in and out with each breath. So the first day back after weeks of injury, I was in another injury. There was still two months till my next fight but I didn't have the time or money to be sitting out. I iced it every day and it would pop in and out after a week. Deep breaths would pop it out. Everything was pain. A whole week of hurting when I laughed, spoke up, sat down, got up, went to the restroom. The rib injury ranks up there as one of the worst injuries I took.

I was out of sparring for five weeks and I was three weeks away from my next fight. I had all this local hype and I needed to be in there. I dug up an old rib protector at the gym and wore it when I worked out to see if it would work. It smelled of death. It came from the community gear tub at the gym. I took it home and bleach washed it. It saved me for the fight. It was a sturdy shell rib protector and wasn't bulky. I used it for the last two weeks.

I don't spar on the week of a fight.

There I was 2-0 with two KO's. The city paper did a story on me and I got a little hometown thing going on. I hadn't taken a shot on my now exposed rib. After the healing I guess the cartilage built up around my top left rib and it stuck out. If I laid on my stomach it would hurt. I wondered what would happen when it got hit without the rib protector. There was only one way to find out.

That was my career though, always fighting hurt. I think

it made me mentally tough and has definitely spilled over into my work now as a coach. Now when my fighters complain, I give them the old man's spiel about how back in my day I used to walk to school in the snow...

I was in the back before the bout. Of course the commission, doctors, everyone was late. They were over an hour late. It's actually quite ridiculous how many times this happens across the USA. I was laying down and scrolling through Facebook and found out that the man that always kept me in good spirits, my trainer, and friend Apidej, had passed away from his long battle with cancer earlier in the day.

I was devastated. I had planned on going back later that year to visit my old work and say hello to everyone. Most importantly I wanted to see Apidej and his son Neung, who would always corner me.

I didn't know what to do. I was in Texas, not in Thailand. I didn't know if I should call someone in the family. I just started pacing around the changing area. I wasn't thinking at all of my fight. Suddenly as I stopped pacing, I felt something divine, spiritual, something outside of me really hovering over me. I felt a higher power. I felt a burning sensation in my chest as my trainer called me over to get my hands wrapped. I no longer thought about my rib injury through camp. I was only thinking about honoring my teacher that night.

I could see Apidej smiling and telling me to, "go running and hit pad with me."

I shadow boxed and told my trainers that my Thailand trainer had passed away today.

"Let's get this guy outta there for him," they simply said.

I had the best boxing coaches. They were all experienced and were the seen it all types. I never wanted to show I was off.

I put on my gloves and made my way to the ring.

The bagpipes started and I was on the way to the ring with the local crowd going crazy. I just saw them all jumping, clapping, and yelling but I didn't hear anything. Everything was so quiet in my head, I was bouncing in my corner and could see the announcer pointing at me and saying my name but not a sound. My chest was still burning. I usually talked to myself in my head before a fight. I repeat strategy, I repeat how I am going to win, but this time I simply wasn't thinking a thing, or hearing a thing for the first time in all my fights.

It was silence.

Then the bell rang and I landed a hard jab that stumbled my opponent. I went right after him. He was in trouble right away. He ate a few uppercuts and held on for dear life. The ref broke us and the next onslaught the ref came in to wave it off as my opponent was still standing. I wasn't excited. I just walked toward my corner.

My hearing slowly came back and the crowd appeared as I congratulatory bumped gloves with my trainers. The referee raised my hand and I heard the bagpipes, the crowd, and I made my way to the back. I got pulled aside by the production crew that was filming the fights for an interview. They did the usual; how did you feel coming into the fight? I finally was able to talk and show some sort of emotion.

"My Muay Thai trainer and legend Apidej Sit Hirun passed away today, this fight was for him, I could feel him before the fight, man I wanted to deliver for him," I said. I *wai'd* to the camera.

I took no damage at all. I didn't get my rib touched. I sat down and just took in what was an experience. My opponent wasn't some world beater, but I had overcome a neck injury, probably a broken rib, and the sad news of my trainer passing in Thailand. I took a knee and gave thanks, and really sat there for a second. I wasn't sure I wanted to be around everyone after that. I hung in the back for a little bit and eventually made my rounds out to the crowd hidden in a hoodie.

A few days went by and I wasn't able to get much information on Apidej's funeral processions. I had some of his family on Facebook but a lot was in Thai and I was not able to communicate well with them.

I felt bad because I wasn't there. I still think about it. Sadly, I can't remember what our last interaction was. When I was working my last days at Fairtex he was away with illness for a time. I always just thought I could go back to the camp anytime and pay him a visit.

15

RETURN TO MUAY THAI

I had three professional boxing fights in five months and won them all by KO. Life was pretty good. I was teaching Muay Thai, maintaining my boxing, training Andrew Craig and traveling.

My first real camp with Andrew he had a crazy come from behind head kick KO over Rafael Natal at a UFC. I cornered him for the fight in San Jose. I didn't work with many MMA athletes at the time. Striking was the last priority at the time for them. They all thought that doing pads two or three times a week would prepare them well for their fight. They needed to be in classes doing drills, getting in reps and sparring as well. Andrew was one of the few that listened and it worked well.

The whole atmosphere of fight week stood out to me. There were fans at the elevator wanting pictures, autographs. I hadn't been in an environment like that since I was traveling with my first martial arts coach UFC legend Yves Edwards.

It's a lot of pressure as a coach. You want to say the right thing all the time, give the correct advice because you're televised. You don't want to say anything stupid.

I started to find I really enjoyed training fighters. During the camps with Andrew it made me remember techniques and ideas. I started incorporating them into my training as well, but also thinking about why I hadn't been using them. It all went back to being away from Thailand.

But it was during that time of coaching Muay Thai to Andrew that I started getting the bug again for Muay Thai.

We worked together for the Natal fight in July 2012, and then took a tough loss to Ronnie Marks in Brazil in January 2013 where he nearly finished him in the closing seconds of the fight. After that we had one of our best camps for Chris Leben. We hit pads two times a day, six days a week, and would end with some good clinch sessions. It was great for me. We didn't have to change our stances worrying about takedowns or anything; we trained like Muay Thai fighters and it paid off. Andrew beat him in what I thought was a clear victory but he only won by split decision.

Judging in MMA is the same as all combat sports, there's a lot of people that aren't experienced in the sport itself making decisions. It's easy to see in boxing, there are judges making decisions about high level fights and people's income on the line.

After that fight Andrew was having trouble finding quality training partners his size in Houston for his next bout which was Luke Barnatt in Manchester, England.

He was traveling to Austin and a lot to Colorado.

It was during the preparation for the Barnatt fight that I got a message from a promoter, Kim Ip, of a show I always wanted to compete on, he was reaching to see about fighting on his show. I always liked his shows because it had top athletes on there Kulebin, Madsua, Colossa, etc. They had great production, great posters, and their WMC Grand Prix title belt held a lot of prestige.

The shows were famous for having one night tournaments in Hong Kong with some of the most competitive weight classes.

"When's the next grand prix," I asked.

"It's at 72kg. You want in?"

I hadn't been at that weight in a long time. All my boxing matches were at middleweight and super middleweight.

I needed it. I was in decent shape from the camp we had for Leben, and my boxing was as sharp as it ever was from the professional boxing stint I had.

"I'm in," I told him.

I was about 15 months removed from my Glory disaster and felt I just couldn't go out like that in Muay Thai or Kickboxing. I also knew that I couldn't do all of my camp in Houston. My date was set for October 21st in Hong Kong and Andrew's October 26th in Manchester. The plan was for us to train together and then 10 days before my bout in Hong Kong I was going to go to Thailand for some fine tuning. After my fight I was going to fly straight over to Manchester and corner him in his fight.

Andrew and I trained together a lot when he was in town and when he was away I worked on my boxing. I told him that I was going to go to Thailand for 10 days before I headed over to Hong Kong.

"Who will corner you," he asked.

"One of the Fairtex trainers is in Hong Kong now working there," I told him.

A few of the trainers actually worked with me when I was the manager at Fairtex and all the others I knew from them visiting. This was also good because this put me in favor with the promoter and saved him money on flying me over a corner. To all you up and coming fighters out there, try to save the promoter money. It helps.

I arrived in Bangkok and got to training at Muay Thai Plaza 2004. I told Mr. Pong that I needed to finish up camp just before I fought in Hong Kong and he lined me up with a couple good trainers. One was the pad man for Saiyok who at the time was running through everyone. Seeing him hit the pads before me got me zoned in. His flow with the trainer was something to see. Every morning I would take a nice walk through the city over to Lumpini park by the old Lumpinee stadium. At that time, it was still up. The best fought there and walking past it and seeing the signage always inspired me. Every morning I ran in the cleanest air in Bangkok. Lumpini park is probably the best run one can have in that city still to this day. I had a great 10 days in Thailand and felt the best I had felt since living in Thailand.

When I got to Hong Kong, I met my driver with no problems. I got to the hotel and it was a day before weigh in. I checked the test scale and I was over by two pounds. So I put on a sauna suit and went down to the fitness room. I did a light jog for about a mile and a half and figured I was good, because sweat was coming off pretty easy. I went back up and it was very close to official weigh in.

I checked and I was half a pound over!

"Damn it," I said aloud.

I went back downstairs in my suit and pumped out a quick mile and went back upstairs. I was good. I had some water and one of my favorites, the Japanese electrolyte drink called "Pocari Sweat."

After the weigh in I wanted to eat but they needed some additional promo pictures for the show the following day. The shoot was before weigh in but I was busy cutting a couple pounds. I did the normal fight pose shots and the sideways shots and then they brought over a briefcase. They opened it up and it was the WMC I-1 Grand Prix belt I was fighting for. I was laser focused. I wanted it.

"Hold it up," the photographer said. "We need to get a shot."

I really didn't want to because I felt I shouldn't be touching something like that until I earned it. The photographer noticed my hesitation.

"Come on, do it."

I did. I didn't like taking a photo with a belt. I wanted it to be something earned.

I had some food tickets which were given to me at the hotel and so I went to the buffet. If you've ever been to China they don't really follow queues or lines, and after a weight cut and photo shoot, I put my hand on a couple men's shoulders and shook my head no when they tried to pass me in line. The buffet food wasn't too great but it did its job. I went up and rested for a bit and messaged some of the trainers.

The gym was having some sort of party or someone from the gym was having a party and they all couldn't get free from it. I knew everything was going too well anyway for the trip. So I let the promoter know and he said one of his friends who was also part of the Hong Kong Muay Thai Federation would help corner me.

"No problem. I'll take anything," I told the promoter.

The next day at the venue we went out and did a walk through. The whole venue was nice. There were tables like those ballroom boxing shows you see in America. The 12 person tables had nice plates and fancy glasses. I reached over to a table and saw they had really nice programs. It had features of all the fighters in the Grand Prix, I made sure I grabbed a couple.

In the back I saw so many friends working corners. At the time Mosi and Colossa from the Challenger were working at the same gym as The Challenger winner Tum Madsua from Thailand. They were cornering alongside Tum's brother in the grand prix. I knew whatever draw I had, if I got him it was going to be tough. He was a two time Thailand King's Cup Champion and The Challenger Muay Thai Reality show winner.

The other two in my tournament were a Canadian Z-1 World Champion who had been living in Thailand for a long time and owned a gym with his wife, and a German champion who was training at Kaewsamrit gym. I had my hands full.

I met up with my trainers and they told me that I had Germany first. I was glad it wasn't Madsua first but also knew he was coming. This wasn't an easy task. Of course he had more experience than me but he was also the biggest guy I have ever fought! He stood around 6 feet 4 inches. We got ready and headed toward the walkout and watched Madsua effortlessly beat the Canadian. The Canadian was good too, but no match for Madsua.

We made our way to the ring and I was feeling good. Round one started and it was very back and forth. I was finding out that I could land solid punches and kicks but when I was close he would hit knees on me and was spike-elbowing me every time we clinched with his height. It was a close round that could have gone either way.

Round two the action picked up really well and I was finding a home with my boxing. I was landing liver shots, and landing clean right hands. I hit an overhand that dropped him but he was up like it didn't hurt him. I mean it wasn't a flash or anything. He was down and took the eight count but he came right back at me. He landed teeps to my face with his length and long knees that were killing my body. Towards the end of the round I caught a kick and hit a big sweep on him. As the round was coming to an end I landed another heavy right hand that dropped him…. but he got right to his feet.

Between rounds two and three my corner told me I had the match already, relax and don't take damage.

"Get ready for the next fight," they said.

The problem was I have never been able to play great defense. I went out for the third round and immediately ate a big teep to my face. I was getting worked heavy in the clinch too. I finally hit a nice dump to slow down the onslaught of knees and spike elbows. His corner is calling for him to clinch me up again and he does and but before he gets a knee off I land a nice elbow. It didn't faze him and he began kneeing my body. We break a couple times and at this time I am just trying to body lock him to get out of there. My head was split up top and my body hurt. Seconds left in the fight and he landed another huge long right knee to my ribs. It was pinpoint to where I separated my ribs a year ago in boxing. I could barely breathe as the bell sounded. It hurt to even raise my hands but I did so with a smile. I knew I had it but I also knew all my castmates and Madsua just saw me take a lot of damage.

I was announced the winner and immediately got taken back to the back to try and repair myself for the next fight.

My top rib had already stuck out from previously separating it but now it looked gnarly. One of the trainers immediately put an ice pack on it and then a towel over the top of my head where I had been cut. Then an ice pack on that. I was sitting in a chair in the middle of both the blue and red corner visibly battered. Colossa and Mosi both came by and told me good fight Michael, which made me feel good. Colossa fought me twice and Mosi had seen me in person lose to him twice by TKO. It was good to get their respect because they were both good champions.

A few bouts went by and I was thinking to myself this could be the last time I ever fought for a world title.

"I gotta get up and start moving," I told myself.

I took the ice packs off and started moving around a little bit. I was honestly not good. I played it off, but my head was pounding and my rib was killing me. It hurt to breathe in and out.

The music hit and I remember thinking I was going down that aisle like nothing was bothering me. I walked down with this angry look and a sense of urgency to go. When the bell rang it was like a lion on a wounded gazelle. Madsua teeped me right in my ribs and immediately went to body shots, when I covered from body shots I got hit with elbows, when I locked him up to clinch. I got tossed. Repeat that through a couple times and add a couple knockdowns. That was the end.

Someone is going to watch just that final fight and see me get completely owned but not know anything I endured before that match. The promoter and sponsors all came in the ring and about 15 ring girls game in. They presented me with a medal and a gold cup and Madsua the WMC I-1 World Championship and a championship robe.

"You got a good heart," the crowd told me.

"You're welcome back anytime," the promoter said.

I wasn't happy with the final but I got close. I got to fight for a world title in Hong Kong against a high level Thai. Yeah I got scorched, but hey.

After the show the promoter took all the athletes to a bar they completely rented out. It was like a house. All the drinks and food were taken care of. I always liked talking to all the camp owners and fighters at those things. Those were where you made your next move or made moves for your friends in upcoming bouts. You make friends with all these people and you always have a place to go when you're in all different parts of Thailand.

The next day I was on a flight to England with a gold cup, black eye, stapled head, and bruised ribs. I arrived and everyone was pumped about how I did.

"It's not like that. No man I lost," I told Andrew. "Let's get you ready."

For a couple days we worked on some stuff and it was fight time again.

Andrew was fighting in enemy territory. He was fighting an Englishman in England. I love Andrew but something just was off in that fight. It could have been the height but he seemed like he never hit his groove. Mind you his opponent was about 6'6 in the middleweight division. The fight was super entertaining and both landed some great shots but Andrew's opponent got the better of the exchanges and clipped him in round two and then secured a choke.

He was down. I was down too. It was the first time as a coach I felt I could have done more as a coach to better prepare, but I went off and did a fight. I think he understood that too. For him to perform at a UFC level, he needed to go to a camp with everything on site. His gunslinger ways got him fight of the night bonus however and he got something like 20-50k in bonus. That long flight home could have been a lot worse.

When we got home it was the first time we both had some time off and we went and hit the bars and Tex Mex real hard for a bit. It was also getting toward the end of the lease on the fight house. He had met a girl in Austin and was going there a lot for training, and I was at the point where I wanted to open my own gym. We worked together for one more fight and then both were too busy and too far away to continue working together.

Then I began opening my first gym with friend Bob Perez, Houston Muay Thai.

16

COUPLE MISTAKES

I had been teaching at MMA gyms for two to three years since I moved back to the states, and at times I enjoyed it but a lot of times I didn't. I always wanted to have my own gym and pass on my teachings and build a brand. There was only one Muay Thai only gym in Houston and it was

Kru Pongs'. Rumors were circulating that it was going to be closing soon.

I kept asking myself, in a city with the fourth largest population how do we not have a Muay Thai Gym? I thought about it and for some reason I thought that I couldn't single handedly open a gym with just my name. I needed to bring in someone else. I reached out to Bob Perez. He had a gentleman's mustache. The ends twirled and he kept them groomed. He was the man to know for MMA striking.

We had worked together a few times and I knew he had a lot of passion for Muay Thai and carried it over well to his MMA athletes.

"What do you think about starting a Muay Thai school," I asked Bob. "We can sublease out of Lou Savarese's gym."

Bob thought it was an awesome idea.

Both of us put in around $5,000 apiece and Houston Muay Thai was born in August 2014. We started off with around 30 students but quickly grew, as did the reputation of the place. A lot of Houston's best were coming by to get work. I took on all of the managerial aspects of the gym including finances, upkeep etc.

I taught classes every day and starting out, Bob would come on Tuesday, Thursday, and Saturdays. We didn't pay each other for the first two to three months we were open. We were growing but we wanted to leave some money in the account in case something happened.

With all the growth I found that I didn't have much time to train myself as I would like to have had. I was teaching and I was learning a lot about the gym business by signing up for martial arts business consulting groups. I was doing online work with some big time gym owners and going to workshops around the country. It really helped me with growth in the business. I can tell you in those consulting groups I learned more in two months than I did in four years of college.

One day I got a message from my old friend in Thailand Mr. Pong. He told me Thai Fight (one of the biggest Thai versus foreigner) type shows was going to have a Kings Cup spread out over two dates to finish out the year in 2014. The first was going to be on the Princess of Thailand's birthday in Bangkapi and the final in December in Bangkok. It was going to be in the 71 kg weight class.

They were looking for an American. Not only that, they're going to fly over a fighter and a corner man. I had never heard in all my years and even today of a Thai promotion paying to fly over an athlete from the USA and a corner. To top it off the pay was around $5,000 for the first fight. It was an amazing opportunity. Being that I was so busy this was out of the question for me. I started reaching out to some of the top Americans at that weight. I was so mad.

"How much does it pay," everyone kept asking me.

"Who is in the tournament?"

"Oh I have to think about it."

"Fuck that man," I told them. "What is there to think about!? If someone offered me a trip to Thailand with a corner for $5,000 I'll fight anyone in my division."

After about a week I told Mr. Pong no one in the USA was up for the challenge and that I was going to do it. What I was thinking I don't know. My gym just opened a few months prior and how was I going to leave for one or two weeks in Thailand. I told Bob to cover me and he was pumped for the opportunity for me but he wanted to go too.

Instead of reaching out to other coaches and being let down like I was for Glory I reached back out to my old roommate Andrew Craig. Funny thing is this guy has now coached in the first Glory and now the Kings Tournament of Thailand.

Here is where the problem was. I had so many people competing out of the gym and I was training them them with Bob hard. I didn't really train like I should have. The date was getting nearer and I could only afford to be out eight days before the fight. I was in shape cardio wise, but that fast twitch and timing was off from lack of pads and technical sparring. It had been a little over a year since my last Muay Thai bout in Hong Kong.

They announced the eight man lineup and it had some killers in there: Antoine Pinto, Saiyok, Sen Bunthen, etc... All were world champion caliber fighters. Nothing new to me being the least experienced.

We made the trip over and immediately went over to Muay Thai Plaza 2004 gym. What was funny was that Saiyok, Sen Bunthen, and a Brazilian fighting in the Kard Chuek Kings tournament were all there. I could have possibly drawn someone from the same gym, but that's Muay Thai sometimes.

A bunch of media outlets came to the gym one day and we all shot some photos.

"I think you will fight Antoine Pinto," Mr. Pong told me. "In the first round of the tournament."

Antoine had about 150 fights and had lived in Thailand for most of his career. He was a technician but I felt if I could just get my hands on him a couple times I could get him. I couldn't out technique him. I had to make it a dog fight and frustrate him.

Making weight for the fight was easy for me. We showed up at weigh-ins and saw a bunch of familiar faces. Yodsanklai was fighting in the Kard Chuek eight man tournament and I said hello to him and his trainers from Fairtex Pattaya. They were always so nice to me even after I left working at Fairtex. I saw Sasan who helped me land some big fights when I lived in Thailand. It was kind of like a homecoming for me. I was excited. I even talked to Antoine and his family. I had seen them often and fought on the same shows before as him and his younger brother.

After the weigh-in, me and Andrew got some good food and just relaxed but we had to stay at the venue and do a walk through. The royal family was going to be in attendance so they had us do some specific things in our walk out to the ring. First, when the music and introduction began we had to shadow box for a second and then walk over to a huge portrait of the King of Thailand. We were then to *wai* standing in front of him and then hit our knees and *wai* to him there. After that we would make it to the ring and wait for the referee to bring us to the center. The ref would then hold both myself and the opponent's glove and we were to *wai* to the princess of Thailand. It was a long process and not really something you want to do post weigh in but I understood the importance.

I had a normal night's sleep. Ate a good breakfast and made our way over to the arena that was at the top of the Mall Bangkapi and it was done up real nice. It had crazy lighting and sound. I was in the back and was in the same room with Yodsanklai and the Fairtex crew. It was an experience. Saenchai was there along with so many greats it was cool.

I had all my gear on and one of the Thai Fight officials told me I had to wear the Thai Fight anklets. I never liked wearing those but I put them on anyway. As I was sitting down this little cute chubby Thai boy came over to me and just stared at me. I put my fist for a fist bump and he smiled. We took a picture together. As always I was cool and calm before the fight and was trying to remember the routine for paying respects to the royal family.

The music hit and I got everything right going to the ring and inside the ring. I took my time in the *wai kru* and tried to focus. I thought it would be a very challenging fight. As I finished my *wai kru* I totally forgot that Andrew had no idea how to remove the *mongkol* and do a prayer. One of the other Thai trainers that they gave me bumped Andrew and told him to get up the stairs.

"Oh shit Irish what do I do," he said.

Give me some water and put your hands together like you are saying a prayer," I told him.

It was so awkward.

"Now take the *mongkol* off and get the fuck outta here," I said with a laugh.

Round one started and we made a mutual motion to touch gloves and this dude pulled it and teeped me right in the fucking face. I was like man fuck this guy. It was a little bit of a back and forth the first round but I ate a couple left kicks that gave him the round.

Round two started out and he tried running across and doing some crazy shit again. I'm thinking what is going on? Never seen dude fight like this. Well back to work. It was a little more competitive round but again he probably edged it with some clean left kicks again.

"Let's go, it's the last round. Go fuck him up," Andrew yelled at me between rounds.

It wasn't much technical advice but who cares.

Round three began and it was back and forth. Throughout the fight Antoine kept good distance and cut out my front leg when I tried to use my boxing. He also used his left kick well on my arms. At one point he put his long guard out which is when you extend your lead hand out and cover your face with your rear hand. At this point I landed my best punch of the fight, an uppercut! He took a couple steps back and made a gesture with his hands to which I knew I hurt him, but also maybe woke him up a bit.

Shortly after that he came in with an up elbow that

dropped me. I didn't see it. I got up but was still wobbly. He came back at me and hit me with another elbow dropping me. The ref immediately waved it off. I stayed down for a second to see if there was any blood from my nose as both elbows landed flush. My eyes and nose hurt but I got up quickly as Antoine came over to pay respects to me. I was mad as I was seconds away from finishing the fight. They raised his hand we *wai'd* to the Princess and back to the locker I went.

"Good fight America," people told me.

Antoine came to the back and apologized numerous times for what he did in the beginning of the fight.

"Don't worry about that shit. It's a fight," I told him.

I got all my gear off.

"Your fight shorts," one of the staff told me.

In my head I was thinking... "You guys spend money to fly me and my corner, and pay a good purse but won't let me keep my trunks I fought in?"

"Here take them," I said giving the shorts back.

As I was heading out of the arena many people wanted to take photos to my surprise. A couple of old fighting friends Frank Giorgi from the Challenger came by and said good work. For a guy training out of Texas and opening a gym a couple months ago and being out of competition a year since Hong Kong I guess I did alright for Antoine I suppose. I still wasn't happy.

The next day me and Andrew went to a pool party in Bangkok with my face all busted up. We started having a couple drinks and then Mr. Pong messaged me that the money was ready to pick up from the fight. So we left briefly and picked up the money. I paid Mr. Pong a cut and gave some money to the trainers. They were all hanging out at a picnic table with Saiyok. They were all really happy with what I gave them.

"Hey man we can't go back to the party. We got a plane to catch," Andrew said.

I sent Andrew back to the hotel and said I would get back to him closer to the flight. That of course didn't happen.

When I got back to the party I saw my friend who was a former fighter, dj'ing, Zidov Akuma. Then I saw staff from Elite Boxing and some Muay Thai celebrities.

"What the fuck you doing fighting Antoine Pinto," they said. "Aren't you done fighting?"

We all had a good laugh and I made my way back into the madness.

Andrew texted me and said he was heading to the airport.

"I'll see you back stateside," I texted back.

"Man you're crazy," he replied.

I had a good one at the pool party and after party. But I had to face the music and re-book my flight. I just went straight to the airline office at the airport and told them I had just fought and I couldn't fly yesterday. They looked at me like I was crazy because my nose was caved in. They told me that I would have to pay $800 to change my flight.

"Hell no," I said in my head.

I pulled out my phone and took a shot and showed them photos from Thai Fight and they all started changing their tune.

"Wow! Ok I talk to manager," the receptionist said.

The manager came out and switched my flight back home for $150.

Back home I went back to teaching and the grind. Then Legacy Fighting Championships owner and now UFC Matchmaker Mick Maynard reached out to me about having a high level Kickboxing show come back to the Houston area under his brand Legacy. He was going to call it Legacy Kickboxing. I put him in touch with Eric Haycraft to secure some of the Dutch fighters and I helped with some of the matchmaking regarding US fighters. He asked what I thought about fighting on it? I told him I just learned a lesson about trying to train for a fight while running a gym and training fighters.

A couple weeks went by.

"Who do you want to fight," he said.

There weren't any high level pros in Houston at the time for Muay Thai or Kickboxing and he really wanted to showcase me on there. Not one to turn anything down I suggested a rematch with Marco Pique who beat me in his hometown in Paramaribo, Suriname and now this time he can come to my hometown. Plus, he broke my arm. It made for a good story for American audience.

Within a week we had the fight secured. I made the initial conversation in fact.

"Hey what's up Marco," I said over messenger to him. "We gotta run it back in my hometown."

He was cool and said sure thing.

So here is where the problem was again. I was training the fighters that were on the undercard with my partner Bob, and I was still running the gym. I also had just got into a relationship. I mean we were still within the first six months of my gym opening. I thought maybe this would bring a lot of attention to my gym. All the high level guys on the card were going to come by and train, I could maybe use that for promotion of the gym.

There was no "camp" for this. I was just there. I remember about a week before the fight I called one of my students to come up to the gym to drill. I did this for a couple days that was about the extent of my training. I occasionally hit a few rounds with Bob but he was busy too training all of our athletes. We had a four or five athletes on the undercard and with the show in Houston we were all out hustling tickets and getting medicals all ready for everyone.

Well it was fight week and the fighters' hotel was right down the street from the gym. Cosmo Alexandre was taking on Regian Ersel, and me and Marco were re-matching. The card even featured current UFC world champion Valentina Shevchenko. She actually did a lot of her sparring and drilling with athletes from my gym. It was funny Regian and Marco flew over together with a coach and I went to go pick them up to come work out at my gym. I was kind of helping with the show and Marco was a good friend so I didn't think much of picking them up for training. As I've said before, I've never had any ill will toward any opponent. I just like to fight. Regian was young at the time and I remember seeing his face when I picked them up at the hotel.

"You guys talking about food and things to do in the city," Regian said. "This crazy to me y'all are fighting."

"It is kind of weird but fuck it man," I said laughing.

Houston had no clue what kind of talented international card it had. I sold a lot of tickets but people had no idea I was taking on a world champion with over 100 fights. They had no clue who Regian, Cosmo, Pat Barry, Valentina Shevchenko and all the people on the card were. I remember walking out to the fight that I was going to get the Houston card hype by coming out to the Houston classic 'Tops Drop' by Fat Pat. I remember pacing around and waiting for the song to hit but the crowd was quiet. I was like what the fuck; all these new school people here don't know about this classic? They weren't a very good crowd for the kickboxing fights earlier. A lot of booing and non appreciation for high level kickboxing.

I made my way to the ring focused anyway.

Round one started and I was in a groove. I was landing combinations, and landing body kicks, and low kicks. Hell at one point I threw a flying knee. I definitely won the first. I was back in my corner and I was relaxed. Maybe it was fighting at home? I don't know but it didn't last long.

Round two started and I was good too and then I got hit with a grazing overhand on the temple and it just turned the fight. I wasn't seeing anything anymore. My output shut down and was not well. Later in the round I got hit with a knee flush on my jaw and I went down. I was fucked up but I wasn't going out like that.

I survived the round.

In the corner they were debating calling it as I wasn't really there.

"I'm good," I said.

I started round three pretty good and got the crowd going but I got hit with the right again and it was not good. I ended up getting almost to the end and got hit one more time with a right that gave me a delayed reaction. I took two steps and my legs went out. Fight was over.

Two fights in a row getting stopped in the last seconds of the fight. Sure they were against champions but I don't want to be known as some journeyman bum and here I am in my hometown getting rocked.

I remember people saying they were inspired how I would continually keep getting up, and I was thinking, no man I'm just a fighter and I got an ass beating on live nationwide TV and of course I'm getting up.

"You were the hometown guy, why would you bring in someone with four times your experience," my dad's friend from the crowd said later. "Did you think about your gym or your brand?"

I was thinking, "yeah I could have taken on a bum and wasted him but that's just not me, never was."

I was of course embarrassed and had to face my students and my girlfriend and her family. They were all new to this. I just told them I'm good and just tried to avoid talking about it altogether.

I remember re-watching the fight that night and hearing UFC Hall of Famer Pat Miletich give me zero credit in the broadcast.

"Well apparently the film crew think Corley won the first round as they are only showing highlights of him," he said after the first round. "I thought Pique clearly got it."

I was thinking what's wrong with this guy? I clearly won the first round and Pat was sounding like I was some bum. It just added to the embarrassment and frustration. I took a chance. I was a local guy trying to shine with the international elite. I'm not that hungry young man in Thailand living and breathing Muay Thai. I was a gym owner, I was a trainer, I was a manager, I was a matchmaker, and I was done.

17

LAST FIGHT

H ouston Muay Thai was quickly making a name on the scene with me and Kru Bob over the next two years.

We had multiple athletes winning A class division at national Muay Thai and kickboxing tournaments. Our

MMA athletes were excelling at top regional shows. I always wanted to make my students surpass me and some.

During this time as a gym owner and coach I started to get back involved in USA Muay Thai. I had been keeping up with the teams and they seemed to be in the same place as when I was selected. I saw that a team was being put together for 2016 and that there wasn't a coach and I volunteered.

Everyone thought it was a great idea and went as the Head Coach of the USA Muaythai Team in the IFMA World Championships in Jonkoping, Sweden in 2016. It was at that tournament I realized I couldn't just sit back anymore and have our USA Teams picked at the last minute and come to World Championships with a handful of people. When I returned home from those World Championships I decided I was going to do something about it. I ran for president of USMF USA Muay Thai. I was unanimously voted in by the board.

As president, a lot and I mean a lot had to be done to get the USA up to speed. I was just starting my presidency in 2016 and my body was in pain from long time injuries that I prolonged so that I could keep competing.

Since I hadn't fought since January 2015, I thought it was time that I go see a doctor about my hernia that I got in 2011.

The right side of my body was in significant pain. I was a broke gym owner and coach and was paying for insurance but even with the insurance I was looking at $5,000 in surgery costs to get my hernia repaired. When I found that out I dropped my insurance altogether. During my search for an affordable hernia doctor in Houston I came across a doctor that did research hernia surgeries and would pay the patient $200 for the surgery. I was sold. I went in and inquired about it.

"You have a pretty good tear on your right side," the

doctor said." You know you have one on the left too, you know that right?"

I couldn't believe it, but also could believe it.

"I can operate on the right side but I'll hold off on the left," he said.

The doctor was a nice older guy, Hispanic with white hair. He'd gone to my undergrad for college so it all felt like destiny. Fate always plays tricks though.

There of course was a catch to getting paid for a surgery.

"Some of the patients are getting a dissolving implant for pain relief, and others will not be getting any pain relief other than over the counter pain medication," he said.

"I've taken plenty of damage already so I should be good," I told him.

After the operation I was in some pain. The first thing I did was look down at the scar.

"What the hell," I said lying down.

My manhood looked absolutely crazy. Just below a two to three inch scar my manhood was entirely blown up solid purple, blue and black, like a blowfish. I was just a big ball. I was frightened.

"How long is it going to be like this," I said to the nurse.

"Oh just about a week, that's normal," the nurse said.

"No way," I said, shaking my head.

I was able to slowly walk out and into my girlfriend at the time's car. I was at her apartment and rested for a few hours and went up to the gym to check on it. I was crazy.

After two days I had to go back for them to evaluate everyone. They had us on a strict regime of medicine and we had to check in via a cellular device given to us. Because this was research they had to keep everything the same whether we got the medicine or not. When we drove back to the hospital I noticed people were being assisted out of their cars and looking in really bad shape. I mean some serious looking pain. I was cool, I got out of the car on my own and walked in. I know I was tolerant of pain but I still felt some sort of awkward numbness.

I went in and everything was good. I turned in all of my tracking devices and logs and went out of there not ever knowing if I got the implant or not.

Weeks went by and I was able to get around but was really just going through movements. I couldn't really kick, run, or anything for my cardio. I started putting on weight. I was still in pain. My girlfriend at the time was in her last year of medical school and was applying everywhere across the country for her residency.

We were together for about two years and everything was really good but we never put in a scenario of what would happen if she left. She had her Match Day. All the doctors get together and find out where they were going for their residency or fellowship.

She got into her top pick. I was really happy for her but also knew that it was going to be tough making the relationship work.

A month passed by quickly and it was time for her to move to Vanderbilt University in Tennessee for her pediatric residency. I was happy for her but we still didn't talk about how it was going to work. The first three months she was there, I flew out for the weekend a couple times. Something just wasn't the same. I could tell she was overwhelmed with her work and I was getting overwhelmed with my work as a gym owner, and more so president of the USA Muay Thai Federation. I was about to take on my biggest task as an adult and president of the USMF, I was taking over the first ever USA youth team to Thailand. Twenty-two kids from all over the country went with their parents to compete. To say that I was stressed was an understatement.

I was training two of the junior athletes Rebekah Irwin

and her brother Zac Irwin. Due to finances I told the family I would take care of them. So they let their 15 year old daughter and 17 year old son travel with me to Thailand with the USA Youth Team.

The first couple of days were very hectic, trying to coordinate all the kids together at the same place and same time as you can imagine wasn't easy. It was the morning of the second day there that my girlfriend called me and I could tell she had been drinking. I heard other girls in the background and they were all just talking crazy.

"I've been talking to my friends and they told me this just isn't going to work," she said. "It's not and you're not going to change who you are. How many times have I told you to dance with me? Or dance with me at my families get together? How many times..."

I was by the old Lumpinee, near Muay Thai plaza, when that gym was around. I'd been walking around looking for something for breakfast. My stomach dropped as she pounded into me. She let me have it really out of nowhere and that was that. It was pretty poor timing.

I was down for the rest of the day but I had a major job to do. The tournament was seven days long! There were some good and bad stories with the first USA Kids team but overall, it was a success. My fighter Bekah Irwin and Patrick Rivera's student Lauren Cabaug become USA's first youth gold medalists. That made me so happy that it washed away things, temporarily.

I went back home and after the celebration was over for the USA Team, I worked and taught privates. I was in some pain still from the surgery. I had a patch of some bad drinking for a bit, dealing with the pain and the ex. I'm a fighter and we always feel like we can fight our way out of things. Sometimes the best thing is to take an L and move on. It took a little bit.

I finally snapped when I was chilling on the floor of the gym with a styrofoam margarita that I had the front desk girl pick up for me on her way into the gym. They were shitty and wine based. I was just gazing out on the mats and realized that the only thing that could snap me out of this funk I was in, was to fight. Fight. I mean how the hell could I train for a fight while training fighters, running a gym, and being president of the USMF?

I found out the hard way that doesn't work with Pinto and Pique. I had more motivation than ever. Rocking a dad bod from surgery in all the IFMA youth world's photos that had all my Thai friends asking me what happened, and a break up was my fuel.

I called my old friend Mr. Pong and told him what my plan was.

"I just want one more fight," I told him.

"You?"

"Yeah."

"Ok sir," he said.

"I'll be there in 10 weeks."

We decided to go all in with this show. I was going to bring three of my students to compete and I was going to challenge former 2x WPMF World Champion Raseesing. I called Patrick Rivera and he brought one of his up and coming youth as well. The show was going to be a USA versus Thailand on Channel 3 Thailand. It was getting a lot of attention and it was even getting write ups in Thailand's famous Muay Siam magazine. My student Rebekah Irwin was at that time an IFMA gold medalist and she was going to be taking on a famous Thai girl who was Miss Teen Thailand. Also featured on the card was Sylvie Von Duuglas fighting on the USA Team, she has amassed the most fights as a foreigner in Thailand.

I was more focused than I had been in a long time. No

drinking and I was eating pretty good. I couldn't sit still for a lot of nights.

I kept thinking of all the negatives that had happened recently. I kept thinking about the fight. I didn't want to have this last fight and get embarrassed. So three or four nights of the week I would go back to the gym after the gym was closed and hit a 5-5-5. Five Jump rope rounds, five shadow box rounds, and five on the bag. I would have the music blaring. Jacob Rodriguez, my student, would join me for most of these sessions. It was like meditation for me. Moving with the music talking to myself. I knew that this fight I could not be defeated.

I went through all the holidays, my birthday, Christmas, and New year without drinking. I was focused. Time was getting close to departure. From my gym it was going to be my co-owner Bob Perez, my student's mom Angie Sanchez, her daughter Valerie, Rebekah, Jacob, and myself.

For most it was their first time in Thailand, and since I was the one that put it all together I still had to make sure they were all good. Leading up to the fight, along with my training, I was still holding pads for all the fighters along with Bob.

We arrived in Bangkok and with most people being there for their first time I was getting asked a lot of questions.

"When are we going here, when should we do this, what's going on," they repeatedly asked.

It was something I totally didn't think about leading up to the fight but I should have known that not everyone travels across the world for Muay Thai. We went to my old gym Muay Thai Plaza 2004 near the old Lumpinee Stadium but the gym had been bought out by Chinese investors. The quality of training had gone down and there were only two solid trainers. It didn't really matter, we just needed a place to sweat, it was fight week.

In the mornings we jogged together at Lumpini Park and in the afternoon we trained at Muay Thai Plaza. We did that for a couple days and then decided to visit a gym I had taken the kids to for the 2016 World Championship, Numponthep. We got some solid training that day and I got to reunite with one of the old coaches from The Challenger Reality Show, Nugget McNaught from Australia. Nugget is a legendary promoter, fighter and coach.

When I was on the show I was still pretty green and he knew it. He even said it in one excerpt of the show. I think he knew I was more experienced now. I hope I made a better impression on him.

Everyone got some rounds in and everyone was feeling good. We shot some photos and videos that Muay Siam once again shared. It was really cool.

In between sessions I went to the IFMA & World Muay Thai Council headquarters to say hello. They were really happy with how I was growing USA Muay Thai but had a concern with me. They brought me into an office.

"We have been seeing this USA versus Thailand card in the papers and magazines," they asked me. "What are you doing? Can you imagine the President of USA volleyball still competing, or the president of baseball? This is an exhibition right?"

"Exactly! It is an exhibition," I said. "This is the very last one."

After four days in Bangkok we all took a short one hour flight up to Chiang Mai. We all took a taxi over to a cool old style resort. It had a nice pool, and everyone got paired up for rooms.

I had my own room to myself because, hey this was my last fight. Everyone had to make weight so we had to do some serious research to find a sauna in Chiang Mai. There were a couple of steam spots but we were looking for a dry sauna.

Everything was going too good to be true. The promoter told me that my opponent was in a motorbike accident and that they were looking for a replacement.

"It doesn't matter. I'm ready to go," I said.

The next day all of the opponents came to our resort for weigh-ins and photo shoot. Everyone made weight but my opponent and Valerie's opponent weren't there. They told me that I was going to go to the stadium to make sure that they made weight because they were coming in later that day.

Later that evening I went up to see my opponent and he looked like he just walked in and didn't cut weight at all. He weighed in at 71-72kg and the fight was 75kg. I had already put on two kilos at least so I had some significant size on him. I was pretty sure I was going to put on at least another kilo before fight time.

People later on down the road I heard were talking shit about my opponent being undersized. This happens all the time where Thai's come in at their walk around weight and beat the foreigner with their experience. At the time of the fight I had around 30 fights and my opponent had close to 50 wins and around 15 losses. He was also a lot younger and I had not fought in two years and came off a surgery. People will always criticize. He was going to be a challenge regardless.

I got back to the camp and all of us went across the street to the Tesco Lotus food court and ate really well. Jacob sent me a message and told me that he was going to pull from the fight if he didn't change rooms.

"Dude what the hell are you talking about," I messaged back.

"Bob is coughing too much. I can't sleep," he replied.

I had the biggest room so I let him come in. We were talking and I took him through the fight. I said that I saw that my opponent was soft to the stomach and that he was just fighting at his walk weight. I said that I had never finished a fight with a body shot but I was feeling this one.

We got to the arena the next day and everything was rushed. It was big and open air with large high rafters. Most of the people were at the ground level. They had us all get in the ring immediately and they did a bunch of talking and running us through the introduction.

All of a sudden we were live and they talked and introduced both the Thai team and the USA Team and then an elderly man came into the ring and began to sing the USA national anthem, but in the middle of it he forgot the words and just added his own words.

All of the USA athletes chuckled and looked at each other. The Thai anthem finished and we went to the back. The show started with some prelim fights and Patrick and Bob began wrapping hands of Valerie, Bekah, and Jacob. As the hands were getting wrapped my good friend and USA youth coach Rami Ibrahim came up. He was doing a month long camp at Khongsittha in Bangkok but he and camp owner and Thailand celebrity Mathew Deane came all the way up to watch the fight.

It was good that he came; we needed all the hands we could. The fights started abruptly and I was trying to warm up fighters while Patrick, Rami, and Bob either had one of our USA fighters in the ring or right on deck. I didn't get to see any of my students' fight. I was in the back and wrapping Jacob's hands and then a fight would be over and he was gone.

Our team was doing well. Patrick's student won, and then my student Valerie got the wrong end of a decision, Bekah schooled her opponent, and Jacob quickly finished his opponent. I was rushed. I had to wrap my own hands. I had no thai oil massage and no warm up.

This was it, my last fight and just like my whole career things were crazy. I sealed the ring, but I took my time. I paused in each corner and I made the cross in each corner pad. I did my *wai kru* and they brought us to the center of the ring. I had significant size from weigh in to now fight time.

The bell rang and I ate a teep as I pumped out a couple of jabs. I threw a switch kick and BAM! I felt my partial hernia on my left side go. It hurt. I had to block it out. In my head at that moment I was like shit...this is it, this is the end. God wouldn't want me to have an easy last fight. I started using a lot of hands and it was effective.

Occasionally I got hit but round one was all me.

I came back to the corner and told them about my hernia.

"I gotta get this thing over with," I said.

They said some stuff but honestly I couldn't hear them. I was in pain. I was in some zone. I got up off the stool and the second round began. He started to press me a lot more. I landed some good kicks and punches but he was trying to get the clinch. He started taking control in the middle of the round. He caught my kick twice and dumped me both times. At one point I had his face framed away and he swept me from there. I got up and put my glove out to say hey nice one and he wasn't having it. He threw a teep and I caught it over-under and passed it through and threw my hardest liver shot I've ever thrown and it landed flush. He took two steps and dropped in pain.

I knew right when it landed it was over. He rolled on the ground and actually stayed on the ground for two minutes, and needed to be assisted out of the ring. Rami came into the ring and lifted me up. It felt great to win. I knew that there was a higher power with me in that fight. It is why I don't think I could ever do another fight. It was definitely a sign.

I knew that was the end. I knew my body couldn't fight again. I didn't have the fast twitch and the same reactions anymore. I was seeing things great but my body just wasn't responding.

After the fight we were all happy. The USA team got a big trophy and they gave it to me. The USA had beat Thailand in the event and it was all on CH 3 Thailand. The promoters and film crew took us all to eat and it was a great time. We had some good Thai food and of course some Leo beer. I couldn't think of a better way to end my fight career than with a win and my students doing great.

That night before I went to bed I thought about all the hard work I put in, and how it helped me overcome everything in my personal life. I was happy. I won.

18

CONCLUSION

I never won a world title or any real title for that matter in my time fighting. I took on 11 world champions in Muay Thai and of those 11, fought two of them twice. Won some and lost some and left with more victories than defeats. I got to travel the world as a fighter and now I travel even more as a coach.

This journey allowed me to hang glide over the beaches of Rio De Janeiro, go to an elephant sanctuary in Chiang

Mai, ride camels in the desert of Dubai, explore Peru, and walk the beaches of Turkey.

Muay Thai has been rough on me but it's made me a better coach for it. It's got me through some dark times in my life. My fighters don't have to go through all the craziness I did. I love this sport, and I remain a student of it.

As I write this, I am getting ready to run my second four year term as president of the USMF. Giving kids and young adults the opportunity to grow through international competition has been very fulfilling as I know firsthand how it can change your life. I've come to grow with some of these athletes from when they were taking their first trip out of the USA to now winning medals at world championships, or getting signed to major promotions.

My own in-house fighters have already surpassed me. My top student Bekah Irwin has won three gold medals at the IFMA youth world championships, won a Muay Ying world title in Thailand and was the youngest fighter to ever sign to Glory. Speaking of Glory, I fought in the very first one and did awful and since have had Jacob Rodriguez fight and win for Glory at Madison Square Garden against the number six ranked fighter in his debut, and Bekah has won her first three fights in Glory at just 19.

I have also produced many North American Open Champions. Some have gone to Thailand to give it a go, but quickly found out it's not for everyone.

I've opened my own gym, Heritage Muay Thai, where I am trying to teach the next crop of fighters to take my spot. I'm passing on my teachings and just keeping it going.

I'm only 36, and I have many more goals to attain in the sport.

Through the losses I grew stronger mentally and physically. We all aren't put on this earth to be world champions, but I know I'm here to build them.

19

THANK YOU

"Thank you, God, for everything in my life. The good and the bad. Some were blessings and some were lessons." —Anonymous

I WANT to acknowledge and thank the many people that helped me along this Muay Thai Journey. Some of these people I've lost contact with but I still would like to recognize them.

My family for always being supportive even in times it seemed questionable.

My father for instilling a hard work ethic.

All the teachers and coaches that have helped me along the way: Gary Pena, Yves Edwards, Saekson Janjira, Joe Martinez, Lewis Wood, everyone at Fairtex especially Neung, Apidej Sit Hirun, and Jongsanan, Mr. Pong MTP 2004, Bobby Benton, and Lou Savarese.

Organizations and businesses that helped me get valuable experience and assisted in my development: USMF, MTAT, IFMA, Fairtex, Savarese Promotions, and WMC.

Fairtex:

Mr. Wong although a hard man, I learned so much from him and am grateful for all his knowledge.

Ted Okuno at Fairtex Pattaya for getting me opportunities to compete and keeping me level headed when things got crazy.

Chano Nurmakin for helping with the camp and giving me opportunities to be in catalogs and videos.

The former Fairtex president for assisting with my hiring at Fairtex Bangplee.

All the trainers and fighters young and old that helped me in my training.

Bob Perez for jumping in with me on the idea of Houston Muay Thai. In a very short amount of time, we were training high level champions across 3 sports Muay Thai, Kickboxing, and MMA. What we accomplished in 3.5 years is crazy.

Kevin Ross for setting the bar high for Americans. When he was the first American to fight in the Toyota Cup in Thailand I knew I had to do everything I could to get to that opportunity.

Cyrus Washington was one of the top foreigners living and fighting in Thailand at the time I was living there. He was fighting all the time. I had a lot of respect for what he was doing, and we helped each other with fights.

Every athlete and coach that I have worked with on the many USMF adventures around the World.

Thanks Matt Lucas for your patience.

All my students past and present.

I know I forgot some, and I promise to get you on the next book!

Additional photos courtesy of:

Thongchai Anita, Florence Lee, IMAGINE GROUP, Rob Cox, KC Lau, Freddy Sosa, Airdog Photography, and Sam Wong.

Printed in Great Britain
by Amazon

24337191R00096